**St. Louis Community
College**

Library

5801 Wilson Avenue
St. Louis, Missouri 63110

BLACK IMAGE

Kennikat Press
National University Publications
Series in American Studies

BLACK IMAGE

European Eyewitness Accounts Of Afro-American Life

edited by
Lenworth Gunther

National University Publications
KENNIKAT PRESS   //   1978
Port Washington, N. Y.   //   London

To Amy

Manufactured in the United States of America

Published by
Kennikat Press Corp.
Port Washington, N. Y. / London

Library of Congress Cataloging in Publication Data
Main entry under title:

Black image.

(National university publications) (Series in American studies)
Bibliography: p.
Includes index.
1. Afro-Americans—Public opinion—Addresses, essays, lectures. 2. Slavery in the United States—Public opinion—Addresses, essays, lectures. 3. United States—Race relations—Public opinion—Addresses, essays, lectures. 4. Public opinion—Europe—Addresses, essays, lectures. I. Gunther, Lenworth.
EI85.B58   301.15'43'30145196073   77-23110
ISBN 0-8046-9188-6

CONTENTS

BLACK IMAGE

ACKNOWLEDGMENTS

I wish to thank Professor James P. Shenton of
Columbia University, the editors of Kennikat Press, and
the staffs of Columbia University's Special Collections and
the Schomburg Library of New York City for their help.
My greatest debt is to my wife, Selma, for her patience
and understanding during the course of this project.

INTRODUCTION

Since 1607 immigrants from the entire world, but primarily Europeans, have come to America in search of a democratic and materially abundant homeland. This endless wave of humanity has in turn fascinated fellow travelers, critics, and journalists who have sought the Horatio Algers from their homelands who have made it from rags to riches.

European views of American society have not always been the sketches of utopia desired by Americans themselves. Most critics have been awed by the gargantuan nature of everything, but also critical of contradictions in the dream. For many the image is one of poverty and wealth, tolerance and discrimination, violence and order, a land of extremes. So distinct has been the history of America in foreign eyes from that created by United States scholars that the latter have responded with outright condemnation at times, explaining the critiques as propaganda, prejudice, and ignorance. In 1954 the authors of the *Harvard Guide to American History* claimed, "Every student will, soon enough, become aware of the gullibility of travelers in strange lands, of their capacity for getting things wrong, of their instinct for automatic praise or automatic censure." Those same individuals, however, used information and impressions gathered by foreigners. That being the case, they reluctantly recognized that " . . . the occasional penetrating analysis by a first-rate mind may give the historian suggestive and far-reaching insights."

Despite prejudices, envy, and political persuasion, European observers of the American scene have contributed a wealth of information and candor about domestic situations and phenomena often taken for granted or ignored by many Americans. Their impressions provide the world with an image of America, and as such form a history of their own with a far-reaching international impact.

Second to material wealth, the subjects of racism and the Afro-American condition have deeply interested Europeans because of the inherent contradictions with the democratic ideal. In addition, the status of blacks has provided them with rationales for the mistreatment of racial and ethnic minorities in their own societies. Ironically, European commentators have had their own misconceptions of blacks and often exemplified the racist thought of their generation. In fact, the American white way has borrowed from European racial attitudes, theories, and practices. Thus, a symbiotic relationship has developed over the years.

European impressions of blacks predate the Afro-American. By the seventeenth century, when most of western Europe participated in the transatlantic slave trade, slavers and merchants had already been exposed to African kingdoms, civilizations of ancient economic and cultural development, for 150 years. Exploration of the Americas and the use of the gun by whites changed the course of history of the "dark" continent. The African, never culturally, physically, mentally, or spiritually inferior to the European, was indeed incapable of matching his military technology. This fact, in conjunction with ethnocentric and xenophobic reactions to a darker race, provided a rationale for economic exploitation. The onslaught was terrifying. Transplanted Africans, in the eyes of the European traveler, were stripped of their languages, their social and religious customs. Only feelings and dreams could survive the impact of slavery. Hope and pain, rebellion and submission found outlets in song, dance, and prayer. Slave traders, masters, and foreigners alike considered these actions to be the only desires of a so-called emotional, uncivilized people.

Other stereotypes of blacks resulted from existing international developments of the nineteenth and early twentieth centuries. The European partition of Africa was explained and based in part on pseudoscientific theories of black inferiority according to brain size, cranial shape, evolution, and notions of bestiality. French, German, and English travelers to the states between 1885 and 1930 characterized blacks, especially those of darker complexion, in light of these ideas. The fear of black "beasts" sexually assaulting white womanhood prevailed in European and American eyes long after the eclipse of slavery in 1865. Whether or not bestial, the Afro-Americans' Western acculturation supposedly made them superior to their African brethren. Every travel book that includes aspects of black life contains descriptions of them as humble, mannerly, and passive. This behavior amazed travelers who saw the harsh racial conditions.

Critics of the Afro-American situation have also focused on captivating aspects of life within black communities. Miscegenation is one such topic. They have been astonished to see multicomplexioned black folk in a country where interracial arrangements were generally prohibited. Lighter-

skinned blacks, closer to the white norms of physical beauty, have nevertheless been favorably portrayed as the most assertive and outspoken of the
race. The literature of slavery and racial thought produced myths of black
bestiality and inferiority. Yet throughout the country, as foreigners revealed,
the mulatto, slave and free, testified to the white fixation for supposed
"beasts." The deprived status of these people, the children and grandchildren of the master, aroused even European criticism of American whites.

Europeans were critical of any attempts to put blacks in a dominant
political position in the South after the abolition of slavery. They traveled
en masse to the black belt to investigate the new order. In general, the
elite of their ranks, a predominant number, frowned upon the Republican
policy of enfranchising uneducated, landless, jobless people in 1867. This
action, they realized, infuriated southern whites to new heights in racial
violence, a phenomenon already on the rise since 1865. The particular
brand of hostility called lynching, committed against blacks in the era
1865-1930, although an obvious fact in American race relations, received
relatively little attention in the journals of travelers. This lack, deliberate
or otherwise, is difficult to understand.

Travelers have closely examined the shift of black folk from rural to
urban centers since World War I and as a whole deplored the housing, job
situation, health, and social conditions of the ghetto, most notably the
black mecca, New York's Harlem. But American whites have not been the
only "tourists" in the swinging spots of the urban "jungle." The image of
the exotic, earthy black haven has been real enough for the foreigner to
make a side stop "uptown."

Interest in black lifestyles and American racism was capped off by the
racial strife of the 1950s and 1960s. The world press spotlighted the rise
of Martin Luther King, Jr., and his passive resistance movement against
jim-crow policy. The fears of a black backlash, sensed in earlier travelers'
accounts, were realized as the marches, sit-down strikes, urban rebellion,
assassinations, and counterprotests transformed the nation into two camps.
Writers buried the stereotypical Uncle Tom and resurrected Nat Turner.
An American horror show revealed itself as blacks struggled against dog-
reinforced police who water-hosed marchers, and thugs who bombed
churches.

European interpretations of black life are as varied as the nature, eras,
and peculiarities of the people who made them. *Black Image* is a collection
of these views, and as such may appear slanted, distorted, and unappealing
to many Americans. The critiques nevertheless form a history of America
that is real for many people of the world.

Americans must be concerned with every image of their society as the world gets "smaller" in the late twentieth century. Distant peoples have looked on for over three hundred years through the eyes of travelers and critics who published their recollections. Two hundred years ago the young United States had a budding reputation as a democracy. Today this image is suspect throughout the world. Democracy must work at home before being shipped abroad. Foreign interpretations show Americans that they have a long way to go to establish a truly egalitarian society.

Black Image is a source book of Afro-American history as seen through the eyes of white Europeans. In all, three perspectives are contained within it: views on blacks, on American whites, and incidentally on foreign white racial attitudes. Twenty-three selections are included, beginning with Cadamosto's impressions of West African life in the fifteenth century and ending with a description of events in the South in 1967–68, a climactic period in the civil rights struggle.

European views of Afro-American life represent but a segment of world opinion; this collection does not purport to cover every area of international criticism.

I

UNKNOWN DESTINY:
THE SLAVE TRADE

*Some of the slaves have been captured in battle,
others are sent by their parents.*

Anonymous Portuguese pilot, 1540

The European traffic in black cargo was initiated by the Portuguese
explorer Antam Goncalvez in 1441. Until 1518 the trade in Africans was
directed to the European continent. But Christopher Columbus's expedi-
tions to the West, beginning in 1492, established the West Indies as the
future center of imperial commerce and colonization. Sixteenth and
seventeenth-century exploits by the Europeans added North, Central, and
South America to the blossoming possibilities of empire. The ineffective
adaptation of the native peoples and limitations of the white indentured
servant class prompted the transatlantic slave trade in the 1500s. The development and expansion of the sugar economies by the mid-seventeenth
century dealt a final blow to African civilizations. Estimates are that over
10,000,000 blacks were exported in the four centuries of the trade. Exact
figures are impossible to obtain. However, estimates are that 500,000 slaves
were brought to America and over 3,000,000 to Brazil alone, with the
others spread throughout the Indies and Americas.

The gun and African complicity with the European against other blacks
were primarily responsible for the success of the trade. Conquered nations
did not have the military power to compete, despite gallant and sometimes
successful attempts at defense. The African middlemen brought slaves
from the interior to the white slavers on the coast in exchange for guns,
supplies, and cheap goods. The operation depended upon these alliances.
Blacks were then imprisoned in the forts (factories) and kept for the arrival
of the cargo vessels. Once aboard, they were chained and tightly packed
below deck. During the two to three months journey the slaves on most
boats were fed twice a day and regularly danced on deck for exercise and
tension displacement to help prevent revolts, a common fear of the all-male
crews.

Treatment of the slaves was harsh and inhumane. Females were at the mercy of the crews despite ship captains' orders prohibiting miscegenation. Male slaves were in no position to prevent these sexual advances. Physical conditions were another sore spot for the enslaved. Healthy slaves were worth more on the auction block, but the circumstances of the voyages overruled the possibility of clean ships. Disease and pestilence aboard ship killed slaves by the dozens on any single trip. They slept in coffin-like spaces, were forced to lie in their own wastes, and often suffocated during rainy seasons when hatches were closed to prevent flooding. Mortality rates varied depending upon many factors. Most ships lost 20 to 30 percent, some landing in port with 50 percent losses. Trading vessels carried between 25 and 400 slaves.

The impact of the trade was devastating on remaining African societies as well as on the people brought to the West. Foreign languages, customs, foods, and religions were introduced to the captives. Crews employed the lash on rebellious ones and thereby established their physical superiority. Different African peoples were mixed together on the boats, thus creating cultural and linguistic problems for any insurrectionary plans. Black against black kept the outnumbered crews in a relatively secure position.

The abolition of the trade by the English and Americans by 1808 was too late to prevent the disarray of African civilizations. Not until the 1880s when slavery in Cuba and Brazil ended were Africans spared the horrors of the slave trade.

ALVISE da CADAMOSTO

1: BLACK LIFE IN SENEGAL, 1468

*They are very courageous and brutal, for in danger
they prefer to be killed rather than to seize the
opportunity of fleeing. . . . They have no fear whatever of death.*

Alvise da Cadamosto (1426-1483), a Venetian merchant and civil servant,
sailed for Portugal during his West African voyages in the 1450s. The following selection written in 1468 recalls a trip to Senegal. The author was particularly interested in the unique customs and rituals of the people.

THE CUSTOMS OF THE BLACKS, AND THEIR BELIEFS

The faith of these first blacks is Muhammadanism: they are not however,
as are the white Moors, very resolute in this faith, especially the common
people. The chiefs adhere to the tenets of the Muhammadans because they
have around them priests of the Azanaghi or Arabs (who have reached
this country). These give them some instruction in the laws of Muhammad,
enlarging upon the great disgrace of being rulers and yet living without any
divine law, and behaving as do their people and lowly men, who live without laws; and since they have converse with none but these Azanaghi and
Arab priests, they are converted to the law of Muhammad. But since they
have had converse with Christians, they believe less in it, for our customs
please them, and they also realise our wealth and ingenuity in everything as
compared with theirs. They say that the God, who has bestowed so many

*The Voyages of Cadamosto and Other Documents on West Africa in the Second Half
of the Fifteenth Century,* translated and edited by G. R. Crone (London, Hakluyt
Society, 1937), 2nd series, no. 80, pp. 31-34, 42-43, 48-51. Reprinted by permission
of the Hakluyt Society.

benefits, has shown his great love for us which could only be if his law were good—but that, none the less, theirs is still the law of God, through which they will find salvation, as we through ours.

These people dress thus: almost all constantly go naked, except for a goatskin fashioned in the form of drawers, with which they hide their shame. But the chiefs and those of standing wear a cotton garment—for cotton grows in these lands. Their women spin it into cloth of a span in width. They are unable to make wider cloth because they do not understand how to card it for weaving. When they wish to make a larger piece, they sew four or five of these strips together. These garments are made to reach half way down the thigh, with wide sleeves to the elbow. They also wear breeches of this cotton, which are tied across, and reach to the ankles, and are otherwise so large as to be from thirty to thirty-five, or even forty *palmi* round the top; when they are girded round the waist, they are much crumpled and form a sack in front, and the hinder part reaches to the ground, and waggles like a tail—the most comical thing to be seen in the world. They would come in these wide petticoats with these tails and ask us if we had ever seen a more beautiful dress or fashion: for they hold it for certain that they are the most beautiful garments in the world. Their women, both married and single, all go covered with girdles, below which they wear a sheet of these cotton strips bound across, half way down their legs. Men and women always go barefoot. They wear nothing on their heads: the hair of both sexes is fashioned into neat tresses arranged in various styles, though their hair by nature is no longer than a span. You must know also that the men of these lands perform many women's tasks, such as spinning, washing clothes, and such things. It is always very hot there, and the further one goes inland, the greater the heat.

MEN CLEAN IN THEIR PERSONS AND FILTHY IN EATING

The men and women are clean in their persons, since they wash themselves all over four or five times a day: but in eating they are filthy, and ill-mannered. In matters of which they have no experience they are credulous and awkward, but in those to which they are accustomed they are the equal of our skilled men. They are talkative, and never at a loss for something to say: in general they are great liars and cheats: but on the other hand, charitable, receiving strangers willingly, and providing a night's lodging and one or two meals without any charge.

HOW THE LORDS OF THE BLACKS OF
THE KINGDOM OF SENEGA FIGHT

These Negro chiefs are continually at war, the one with the other, and also frequently with their neighbours. They wage their wars on foot, for they have very few horses, as these cannot live on account of the great heat, as I have already said. They do not wear armour, for they have none, save round, broad shields (which they make from the skin of an animal called *danta*, which is very hard to penetrate:) for the attack they carry numerous *azanage*, which are their spears. They hurl these very swiftly, for they are great masters at throwing them. These darts have a tip of iron wrought with barbs, made in various styles: so that when they strike, it lacerates the flesh to withdraw them. They also carry some Moorish weapons in the style of a short scimetar, that is, curved: they are made of iron, not of steel, for they obtain iron from the kingdom of Gambra of the blacks beyond, but they cannot make steel. If there is iron in their land, they do not know of it, or are not skilled in working it. They carry also another weapon, a kind of lance similar to our javelin, but they have no other arms. Their combats are very fatal; since their bodies are unprotected, many are slain. They are very courageous and brutal, for in danger they prefer to be killed rather than to seize the opportunity of fleeing. They are not terrified at seeing their companions fall, as though, being accustomed to this, they are not grieved by it; and they have no fear whatever of death.

THE GRAIN AND THE WINE WHICH ARE
PRODUCED IN THE KINGDOM OF SENEGA

No corn, rye, barley, spelt, or vines grow in this Kingdom of Senega, nor from thence onwards, in any regions of the land of the blacks. This is because the country is very hot and without rain for nine months in the year, that is from October to the end of June. Although they have attempted to sow these grains (which they have obtained from us Christians), they will not grow because of the great heat. (Corn requires a temperate land and frequent rain, which this country lacks.) It appears that they grow various kinds of millet, small and large, beans, and kidney beans, which are the largest and finest in the world. The kidney beans are as big as the long hazel nuts familiar to us, all spotted with different colours, as though painted, and very beautiful to the eye. The beans are broad, thin, and of a bright red colour, though there are others white in colour, very beautiful.

They are sown in the month of July, and harvested in September, because during the period of the rains they till the land. They sow and harvest within the space of three months. They are very bad labourers—unwilling to exert themselves to sow more than will barely support them throughout the year. Few trouble to raise supplies for market.

Their method of working is as follows: four or five of them take their places in the field equipped with certain small spades fashioned like mattocks, and advance throwing the soil before them, a practice contrary to that of our labourers who when tilling the soil draw it towards them. These throw it forward with their mattocks, and do not penetrate more than four inches or so. This is their method of agriculture, and since the ground is fertile and rich, it brings forth those things described above. They drink water, milk, or palm wine. This wine is a liquid which flows from a tree similar to, but not identical with, that which bears dates. There are not many of these trees: they give forth this liquid, which the Negroes call *mignol,* almost the whole year. They proceed in this manner: they make three or four gashes at the foot of the tree, from which flows a brownish liquid like the whey of milk, and place gourds beneath to collect it. A tree does not yield a large quantity, about two gourds in a day and a night. It is very good to drink, and is as intoxicating as wine if water is not added. When first collected it is as sweet as the sweetest wine in the world, but day by day it looses its sweetness and becomes sour. It is better after three or four days than at first. I drank it many times during my sojourn in this country, and preferred it to our own. There is not a sufficient quantity of this *mignol* for everyone to have it in abundance, but all have a reasonable amount, the chiefs the greatest. The trees which yield this wine are common to all (that is, they are not the property of a particular person), for they do not have orchards, or own such trees individually. They are all in the forest, common to everyone to tap and to avail himself of the liquor.

A MARKET, AND THE PEOPLE WHO WENT THITHER

Since it fell to me to spend many days on shore, I decided to go to see a market, or fair, at no great distance (from the spot where I was lodged). This was held in a field, on Mondays and Fridays, and I went two or three times to it. Men and women came to it from the neighbourhood country within a distance of four or five miles, for those who dwelt farther off attended other markets. In this market I perceived quite clearly that these people are exceedingly poor, judging from the wares they brought for sale—that is, cotton, but not in large quantities, cotton thread and cloth, vegetables, oil and millet, wooden bowls, palm leaf mats, and all the other articles they use in their daily life. Men as well as women came to sell, some of the men offering their weapons, and others a little gold, but not in any quantity. They sold everything, item by item, by barter, and not for money, for they have none. They do not use money of any kind, but barter only, one thing for another, two for one, three for two.

These Negroes, men and women, crowded to see me as though I were a marvel. It seemed to be a new experience to them to see Christians, whom they had not previously seen. They marvelled no less at my clothing than at my white skin. My clothes were after the Spanish fashion, a doublet of black damask, with a short cloak of grey wool over it. They examined the woollen cloth, which was new to them, and the doublet with much amazement: some touched my hands and limbs, and rubbed me with their spittle to discover whether my whiteness was dye or flesh. Finding that it was flesh they were astounded.

To this market I went to see further strange sights, and also to find out whether any came thither with gold for sale, but altogether, as I have said, there was little to be found.

THE WOMEN WHO DANCE BY NIGHT

The women of this country are very pleasant and light-hearted, ready to sing and to dance, especially the young girls. They dance, however, only at night by the light of the moon. Their dances are very different from ours.

These Negroes marvelled greatly at many of our possessions, particularly at our cross-bows, and, above all, our mortars. Some came to the ship, and I had them shown the firing of a mortar, the noise of which frightened them exceedingly. I then told them that a mortar would slay more than a hundred men at one shot, at which they were astonished, saying that it was an invention of the devil's. The sound of one of our country pipes, which I had played by one of my sailors, also caused wonderment. Seeing that it was decked out with trappings and ribbons at the head, they concluded that it was a living animal that sang thus in different voices, and were much pleased with it. Perceiving that they were misled, I told them that it was an instrument, and placed it, deflated, in their hands. Whereupon, recognising that it was made by hand, they said that it was a divine instrument, made by God with his own hands, for it sounded so sweetly with so many different voices. They said they had never heard anything sweeter.

They were also struck with admiration by the construction of our ship, and by her equipment—masts, sails, rigging, and anchors. They were of opinion that the portholes in the bows of ships were really eyes by which the ships saw whither they were going over the sea. They said we must be great wizards, almost the equal of the devil, for men that journey by land have difficulty in knowing the way from place to place, while we journeyed by sea, and, as they were given to understand, remained out of sight of land for many days, yet knew which direction to take, a thing only possible through the power of the devil. This appeared so to them because they do not understand the art of navigation (the compass, or the chart).

They also marvelled much on seeing a candle burning in a candlestick, for here they do not know how to make any other light than that of a fire. To them the sight of the candle, never seen before, was beautiful and miraculous. As, in this country, honey is found, they suck the honey from the comb, and throw away the wax. Having bought a little honeycomb, I showed them how to extract the honey from the wax, and then asked whether they knew what it was that remained. They replied that it was good for nothing. In their presence, therefore, I had some candles made, and lighted. On seeing this, they showed much wonderment, exclaiming that we Christians had knowledge of everything.

In this country they have no musical instruments of any kind, save two: the one is a large Moorish *tanbuchi,* which we style a big drum; the other is after the fashion of a viol; but it has, however, two strings only, and is played with the fingers, so that it is a simple, rough affair and of no account.

THOMAS PHILLIPS

2: AFRICAN REACTIONS TO THE TRADE

We had about twelve who willfully drowned them-
selves, and others starved themselves to death. ...

Thomas Phillips, a British slave trader, recorded his impressions of
African societies and slaves acquired during a voyage in 1693-94. He re-
called the desperation of Africans and their willingness to die rather than
face the unknown horrors awaiting them.

The Negroes are so willful and loth to leave their own country, that they
have often leaped out of the canoes, boat and ship, into the sea, and kept
under water till they were drowned, to avoid being taken up and saved by
our boats, which pursued them; they having a more dreadful apprehension
of Barbadoes than we can have of hell, tho' in reality they live much better
there than in their own country; but home is home; we have likewise seen
divers of them eaten by the sharks, of which a prodigious number kept
about the ships in this place, and I have been told will follow her hence to
Barbadoes, for the dead Negroes that are thrown overboard in the passage.
    We had about twelve who willfully drowned themselves, and others
starved themselves to death; for it's their belief that when they die they
return home to their own country and friends again.
    I have been informed that some commanders have cut off the legs or
arms of the most willful, to terrify the rest, for they believe if they lost a
member, they cannot return home again: I was advised by some of my

Thomas Phillips, *A Journal of a Voyage Made in the* Hannibal *of London, 1693-1694,*
from England to Cape Monseradoe in Africa . . . (London, Lintot, 1746), pp. 235,
245-46, in John Churchill, *A Collection of Voyages and Travels,* vol. 6 (London,
1732), pp. 187-255.

officers to do the same, but I could not be persuaded to entertain the least thoughts of it, much less to put in practice such barbarity and cruelty to poor creatures, who excepting their want of Christianity and true religion (their misfortune more than fault) are as much the works of God's hands, and no doubt as dear to him as ourselves; nor can I imagine why they should be despised for their colour, being what they cannot help, and the effect of the climate it has pleased God to appoint them. I can't think there is any intrinsic value in one colour more than another, nor that white is better than black, only we think it so because we are so, and are prone to judge favourably in our own case, as well as the blacks, who in odium of the colour, say, the devil is white, and so paint him.

. . . .

When our slaves are aboard we shackle the men two and two, while we lie in port, and in sight of their own country, for 'tis then they attempt to make their escape, and mutiny; to prevent which we always keep centinels upon the hatchways, and have a chest of small arms, ready loaded and primed, constantly lying at hand upon the quarter-deck, together with some grenade shells; and two of our quarter-deck guns, pointing on the deck thence, and two more out of the steerage, the door of which is always kept shut, and well barred; they are fed twice a day, at 10 in the morning and 4 in the evening, which is the time they are aptest to mutiny, being all upon deck; therefore all that time, what of our men are employed in distributing their victuals to them, and settling them, stand to their arms; and some with lighted matches at the great guns that yawn upon them, loaded with partridge, till they have done and gone down to their kennels between decks. Their chief diet is called *dabbadabb*, being Indian corn ground as small as oat-meal in iron-mills, which we carry for that purpose, and after mixed with water, and boiled well in a large copper furnace, till it is as thick as pudding; about a peckful of which in vessels called crews, is allowed to 10 men, with a little salt, malgretta, and palm oil, to relish; they are divided into messes of ten each, for the easier and better order in serving them; three days a week they have horse beans boiled for their dinner and supper, great quantities of which the "African" company do send aboard us for that purpose; these beans the Negroes extremely love and desire, beating their breasts, eating them, and crying Pram! Pram! which is, Very good! they are indeed the best diet for them, having a binding quality, and consequently good to prevent the flux, which is the inveterate distemper that most affects them, and ruins our voyages by their mortality. The men are all fed upon the main deck and forecastle, that we may have them all under command of our arms from the quarter-deck, in case of any disturbance; the women eat upon the quarter-deck with us, and the boys and girls upon the poop; after they are divided into messes, and appointed their

places, they will readily run there in good order of themselves afterwards;
when they have eaten their victuals clean up (which we force them to for
to thrive the better), they are ordered down between decks, and every one
as he passes has a pint of water to drink after his meat, which is served
them by the copper out of a large tub, filled beforehand ready for them.
When they have occasion to ease nature, they are permitted by the centinels
to come up, and go to conveniency which is provided for that purpose, on
each side of the ship, each of which will contain a dozen of them at once,
and have broad ladders to ascend them with the greater ease. When we
come to sea we let them all out of irons, they never attempting then to
rebel, considering that should they kill or master us, they could not tell
how to manage the ship, or must trust us, who would carry them where
we pleased; therefore the only danger is while we are in sight of their own
country, which they are loth to part with; but once out of sight out of
mind: I have never heard that they mutiny'd in any ships of consequence,
that had a good number of men, and the least care; but in small tools where
they had but few men, and those negligent or drunk, then they surprised
and butchered them, cut the cables, and let the vessel drive ashore and
every one shift for himself. However, we have some 30 or 40 Gold Coast
Negroes, which we buy, and are procured us there by our factors,* to make
guardians and overseers of the Whydaw negroes, and sleep among them to
keep them from quarreling, and in order, as well as to give us notice, if
they can discover any caballing or plotting among them, which trust they
will discharge with great diligence; they also take care to make the Negroes
scrape the decks where they lodge every morning very clean, to eschew any
distempers that may engender from filth and nastiness; when we constitute
a guardian, we give him a cat of nine tail as a badge of his office, which
he is not a little proud of, and will exercise with great authority. We often at
sea in the evenings would let the slaves come into the sun to air themselves,
and make them jump and dance for an hour or two to our bag-pipes, harp,
and fiddle, by which exercise to preserve them in health; not withstanding
all our endeavor, 'twas my hard fortune to have great sickness and mortality
among them.

---

*Factors were Europeans who lived on the African coast and served as middlemen in
the slave trade, acquiring the slaves from sellers and holding the lot for the slavers to
arrive off the coast. (Editor's note)

3: SLAVE MUTINY

*... When they are carried to the plantations, they
generally live much better there, than they ever did
in their own country.*

William Snelgrave, one of many English slave traders of the eighteenth
century, believed the trade to be advantageous to the enslaved people he
considered primitive. The trade, however, had its unsettling moments for
the author, most notably during black rebellion aboard ship.

Several objections have often been raised against the lawfulness of this
trade, which I shall not here undertake to refute. I shall only observe in
general, that tho' to traffick in human creatures, may at first sight appear
barbarous, inhuman, and unnatural; yet the traders herein have as much to
plead in their own excuse, as can be said for some other branches of
trade, namely the Advantage of it: And that not only in regard of the
merchants, but also of the slaves themselves, as will plainly appear from
these following reasons.

First, It is evident, that abundance of captives, taken in war, would be
inhumanly destroyed, was there not an opportunity of disposing of them
to the Europeans. So that at least many lives are saved, and great numbers
of useful persons kept in being.

Secondly, when they are carried to the plantations, they generally live
much better there, than they ever did in their own country; for as the
planters pay a great price for them, 'tis their interest to take care of them.

William Snelgrave, *A New Account of Some Parts of Guinea, and the Slave Trade*
(London, J. Wren, 1754), pp. 160–62, 164–72.

Thirdly, by this means the English plantations have been so much improved, that 'tis almost incredible, what great advantages have accrued to the nation thereby; especially to the Sugar Islands, which lying in a climate near as hot as the coast of Guinea, the Negroes are fitter to cultivate the lands there, than white people.

Then as to the criminals amongst the Negroes, they are by this means effectually transported, never to return again; a benefit which we very much want here.

In a word, from this trade proceed benefits, far outweighing all, either real or pretended mischiefs and inconveniences. And, let the worst that can, be said of it, it will be found, like all other earthly advantages, tempered with a mixture of Good and Evil.

. . . .

The first mutiny I saw among the Negroes happened during my first voyage in the year 1704. It was on board the *Eagle* Galley of London, commanded by my father, with whom I was a purser. We had bought our Negroes in the River of Old Callabar in the Bay of Guinea. At the time of their mutinying we were in that River, having four hundred of them on board, and not above ten white men who were able to do service: For several of our ship's company were dead, and many more sick; besides, two of our boats were just then gone with twelve people on shore to fetch wood, which lay in sight of the ship. All these circumstances put the Negroes in consulting how to mutiny, which they did at four o'clock in the Afternoon, just as they went to supper. But as we had always carefully examined the men's irons, both morning and evening, none had got them off, which in a great measure contributed to our preservation. Three white men stood on the watch with cutlaces in their hands. One of them who was on the forecastle, a stout fellow, seeing some of the men Negroes take hold of the chief mate, in order to throw him over board, he laid on them so heartily with the flat side of his cutlace, that they soon quitted the mate, who escaped from them, and ran on the quarter deck to get arms. I was then sick with an ague, and lying on a couch in the great cabin, the fit being just come on. However, I no sooner heard the outcry, "that the slaves were mutinying," but I took two pistols, and ran on the deck with them; where meeting with my father and the chief mate, I delivered a pistol to each of them. Whereupon they went forward on the booms, calling to the Negroe men that were on the forecastle; but they did not regard their threats, being busy with the centry (who had disengaged the chief mate), and they would have certainly killed him with his own cutlace, could they have got it from him; but they could not break the line wherewith the handle was fastened to his wrist. And so, tho' they had seized him, yet they could not make use of his cutlace. Being thus disappointed, they endeavored to throw him overboard, but he held fast by one of them that they could not do it. My father seeing this stout man in so much danger, ventured amongst the Negroes, to save him; and fired his pistol over their heads, thinking to frighten them. But a lusty slave struck him with a billet so hard, that he was almost stunned. The slave was going to repeat the blow, when a young lad about seventeen years old, whom we had been kind to, interposed his arm, and received the blow, by which his arm-bone was fractured. At the same instant the mate fired his pistol, and shot the Negroe that had struck my father. At the sight of this the mutiny ceased, and all the men-Negroes on the forecastle threw themselves flat on their faces, crying out for mercy.

Upon examining into the matter, we found there were not above twenty men slaves concerned in this mutiny; and the ringleaders were missing, having, it seems, jumped overboard as soon as they found their project defeated, and were drowned. This was all the loss we suffered on this occasion: For the Negroe that was shot by the mate, the surgeon, beyond all expectation cured. And I had the good fortune to lose my ague, by the fright and hurry I was put into. Moreover, the young man, who had received the blow on his arm to save my father, was cured by the surgeon in our passage to Virginia. At our arrival in that place we gave him his Freedom; and a worthy gentleman, one Colonel Carter, took him into his service, till he became well enough acquainted in the country to provide for himself.

I have been on several voyages, when there has been no attempt made by our Negroes to mutiny; which, I believe, was owing chiefly to their being kindly used, and to my officers' care in keeping a good watch. But sometimes we meet with stout stubborn people amongst them, who are never to be made easy; and these are generally some of the Cormantines, a nation of the Gold Coast. I went in the year 1721, in the *Henry* of London, a voyage to that part of the coast, and bought a good many of these people. We were obliged to secure them very well in irons, and watch them narrowly: Yet they nevertheless mutinied, tho' they had little prospect of succeeding. I lay at that time near a place called Mumfort on the Gold Coast, having near five hundred Negroes on board, three hundred of which were men. Our ship's company consisted of fifty white people, all in health: And I had very good officers; so that I was very easy in all respects.

This mutiny began at Midnight (the moon then shining very bright) in this manner. Two men that stood centry at the fore-hatch way, where the men slaves came up to go to the house of office, permitted four to go to that place; but neglected to lay the grating again, as they should have done: Whereupon four more Negroes came on deck, who had got their irons off, and the four in the house of office having done the same, all the eight fell on the two centries, who immediately called out for help. The Negroes endeavoured to get their cutlaces from them, but the lineyards (that is, the lines by which the handles of the cutlaces were fastened to the men's wrists) were so twisted in the scuffle, that they could not get them off before we came to their assistance. The Negroes perceiving several white men coming towards them, with arms in their hands, quitted the centries, and jumped over the ship's side into the sea.

I being by this time come forward on the deck, my first care was to secure the gratings, to prevent any more Negroes from coming up; and then I ordered people to get into the boat, and save those that had jumped overboard, which they luckily did: For they found them all clinging to the cables the ship was moored by.

After we secured these people, I called the linguists, and ordered them to bid the men-Negroes between decks be quiet (for there was a great noise amongst them). On their being silent, I asked, "What had induced them to mutiny?" They answered, "I was a great Rogue to buy them, in order to carry them away from their own country; and that they were resolved to regain their liberty if possible." I replied, "That they had forfeited their freedom before I bought them, either by crimes, or by being taken in war, according to the custom of their country; and they being now my property, I was resolved to let them feel my resentment, if they abused my kindness: Asking at the same time, whether they had been ill used by the white men, or had wanted for any thing the ship afforded?" To this they replied,"They had nothing to complain of." Then I observed to them, "That if they should gain their point and escape to shore, it would be no advantage to them, because their countrymen would catch them, and sell them to other ships." This served my purpose, and they seemed to be convinced of their fault, begging, "I would forgive them, and promising for the future to be obedient, and never mutiny again, if I would not punish them this time." This I readily granted, and so they went to sleep. When daylight came we called the men Negroes up on deck, and examining their irons, found them all secure. So this affair happily ended, which I was very glad of; for these people are the stoutest and most sensible Negroes on the Coast: Neither are they so weak to imagine as others do, that we buy them to eat them; being satisfied we carry them to work in our plantations, as they do in their own country.

. . . I must observe here, that these linguists are natives and freemen of the country, whom we hire on account of their speaking good English, during the time we remain trading on the coast; and they are likewise brokers between us and the black merchants.

ALEXANDER FALCONBRIDGE

4: SEXUAL HORRORS OF THE TRADE

*The officers are permitted to indulge their passions
among them at pleasure, and sometimes are guilty
of such brutal excesses, as disgrace human nature.*

Alexander Falconbridge served as a ship's surgeon aboard an English slave trader and later as a medical relief agent for St. George's Bay Company in the British colony of Sierra Leone. In 1788, four years before his death, Falconbridge published his memoirs of the trade. The author recalls with abhorrence the physical conditions of the slave quarters and the sexual abuse of the women.

The Gold Coast Negroes scarcely ever refuse any food that is offered them, and they generally eat larger quantities of whatever is placed before them, than any other species of Negroes, whom they likewise excel in strength of body and mind. Most of the slaves have such an aversion to the horse-beans, that unless they are narrowly watched, when fed upon deck, they will throw them overboard, or in each other's faces when they quarrel.

Upon the Negroes refusing to take sustenance, I have seen coals of fire, glowing hot, put on a shovel, and placed so near their lips, as to scorch and burn them. And this has been accompanied with threats, of forcing them to swallow the coals, if they any longer persisted in refusing to eat. These means have generally had the desired effect. I have also been credibly informed, that a certain captain in the slave trade poured melted lead on such of the Negroes as obstinately refused their food.

. . . .

Alexander Falconbridge, *An Account of the Slave Trade on the Coast of Africa* (London, J. Phillips, 1788), pp. 28–32.

The women are furnished with beads for the purpose of affording them some diversion. But this end is generally defeated by the squabbles which are occasioned, in consequence of their stealing them from each other.

On board some ships, the common sailors are allowed to have intercourse with such of the black women whose consent they can procure. And some of them have been known to take the inconstancy of their paramours so much to heart, as to leap overboard and drown themselves. The officers are permitted to indulge their passions among them at pleasure, and sometimes are guilty of such brutal excesses, as disgrace human nature.

The hardships and inconveniences suffered by the Negroes during the passage, are scarcely to be enumerated or conceived. They are far more violently affected by the sea-sickness, than the Europeans. It frequently terminates in death, especially among the women. But the exclusion of the fresh air is among the most intolerable. For the purpose of admitting this needful refreshment, most of the ships in the slave trade are provided, between the decks, with five or six air-ports on each side of the ship, of about six inches in length, and four in breadth; in addition to which, some few ships, but not one in twenty, have what they denominate wind-sails. But whenever the sea is rough, and the rain heavy, it becomes necessary to shut these, and every other conveyance by which the air is admitted. The fresh air being thus excluded, the Negroes' rooms very soon grow intolerably hot. The confined air, rendered noxious by the effluvia exhaled from their bodies, and by being repeatedly breathed, soon produces fevers and fluxes, which generally carry off great numbers of them.

During the voyages I made, I was frequently a witness to the fatal effects of the exclusion of the fresh air. I will give one instance, as it serves to convey some idea, though a very faint one, of the sufferings of those unhappy beings whom we wantonly drag from their native country, and doom to perpetual labor and captivity. Some wet and blowing weather having occasioned the port-holes to be shut, and the grating to be covered, fluxes and fevers among the Negroes ensued. While they were in this situation, my profession requiring it, I frequently went down among them, till at length their apartments became so extremely hot, as to be only sufferable for a very short time. But the excessive heat was not the only thing that rendered their situation intolerable. The deck, that is, the floor of their rooms, was so covered with the blood and mucus which had proceeded from them in consequence of the flux, that it resembled a slaughter-house. It is not in the power of the human imagination to picture to itself a situation more dreadful or disgusting. Numbers of the slaves having fainted, they were carried upon deck, where several of them died, and the rest were, with great difficulty, restored. It had nearly proved fatal to me also. The climate was too warm to admit the wearing of any clothing but a shirt, and that I had pulled off before I went down; not withstanding which, by only continuing among them for about a quarter of an hour, I was so overcome with the heat, stench, and foul air, that I had nearly fainted; and it was not without assistance, that I could get upon deck. The consequence was, that I soon fell sick of the same disorder, from which I did not recover for several months.

II

SLAVERY

> *They were fastened up by their wrists to a beam or a branch of a tree, their feet barely touching the ground, their clothes turned over their heads, and their backs scored with a leather thong. . . .*
>
> Frances Anne Kemble, 1839

The first slaves in British America arrived in Jamestown, Virginia, in 1619. These twenty blacks, their descendants, and later arrivals lived in a world of de facto prejudice and discrimination as indentured laborers until their legal status as slaves was confirmed in 1661. Black bondage blossomed in the eighteenth century, spreading into all thirteen colonies by 1749. The institution grew in conjunction with the commercial demand for tobacco, indigo, sugar, hemp, rice, and later cotton. Demand for these crops, as well as the fertile southern soil, were bad omens for the African.

Religious principles, economic and geographic factors, in addition to post-revolutionary war humanitarianism, help explain the decline of slavery in the North and its prohibition in the western territories. By 1804 all states north of Delaware had passed gradual emancipation laws, freeing slaves over a period of time; the number remaining in 1830 was negligible. Circumstances in the South, however, were quite different.

There were 700,000 slaves in the states, mostly in the South, in 1790, the first year of the republic. By 1860 that sum had grown to 3,900,000, an enormous increase when one considers that the slave trade to the United States was illegal by 1808. Importation laws notwithstanding, planters needed more slaves for the growing economy of the newly acquired lands of the Louisiana Purchase of 1803. A domestic trade in surplus slaves from plantations and breeders in the upper South to regions west of Georgia answered the call. The "black belt" was further stocked by an illicit transatlantic trade.

Cotton was "king." Textile mills in the North and Europe needed it, and the slavocrats supplied the goods. The annual production of "white gold" was 12,000 bales in 1792, one year before the invention of the cotton gin. By 1815 and 1860 that figure had climbed respectively to 461,000 and 5,000,000. The burden of this growth was on the Afro-American.

The omnipresent slaveholder is a myth of southern history. South Carolina and Mississippi were the only states to have more blacks than whites and to have 50 percent or more slaveowning families. Most whites in the South (fifteen slaveholding states) in 1860 did not own slaves; only 385,000 families of 1,500,000 had them. In the decade before the Civil War, a minority of slaveholders owned a majority of the slaves, with most plantations having less than twenty slaves, and only 250 units with 200 or more blacks. The mansion on the hill was an exception to the rule. Southern aristocrats held economic and political power far out of proportion to their number. Their social image permeated most white households. Many whites were influenced by the conspicuous consumption of the planter class and had their own delusions of grandeur. A few owned slaves, and many wanted them.

For the slave there was little or no chance of upward mobility out of bondage. Freedom for most was as distant as the north star. Masters were aided by white slave patrols in maintaining social order. Within these established limitations blacks developed their own subculture. Song and dance offered momentary relief and escape from the monotony of field and house work. Men and women tried to their utmost to keep families together in a society that refused them legal recognition. Males were not "legal" heads of households in the eyes of whites, but they were so to their women.

Survival dictated role playing, and blacks became experts, often feigning the "Sambo" personality. Topography, white numerical and military dominance, plantation size, and acculturation processes were deterrents to any successful mass revolt. Day-to-day resistance prevailed as the ultimate expression of frustration and dissatisfaction. This individual rebellion, in the form of crop, tool, and animal destruction and sometimes murder of the master and his wife, clearly indicated no mass docility and submission. The myth of Sambo, the childlike, fun-loving, loyal slave, had its roots in the needs of whites to rationalize slavery and convince themselves that blacks would not revolt.

The impact of slavery on whites and blacks can never be fully gauged. From the nakedness of the auction block to burial in a slave plot on the plantation, blacks weathered a lifelong storm of suffering. An entire people, proud and once independent, were forced to depend on the moods, desires, and actions of the master class. White society adjusted to this population. Civil, political, social, and economic norms reflected the importance of the "slave power." Even Christianity was changed to accommodate the proslavery faction. The paranoid style of southern militarism was caused more by fear of slave revolt than by any frontier considerations.

The stereotyped slave and white images of slaveholding society form only one side of the story, a part revealed by blacks from dawn to dusk. Their lives from dusk to dawn were another matter. Those few hours were enough to rest, storytell, pray, love, plan revolt, and dream of a better day.

HECTOR ST. JOHN CRÈVECOEUR

5: THE LOT OF SLAVES IN CHARLESTON

. . . I perceived a Negro, suspended in the cage. . . .
Birds had already picked out his eyes, his cheek
bones were bare; his arms had been attacked in
several places, and his body seemed covered with a
multitude of wounds.

In 1759 the French writer J. Hector St. John Crèvecoeur (1735–1813)
settled in upstate New York, establishing himself as a farmer and social
critic. Despite American naturalization in 1765, Crèvecoeur spent most of
his later years, 1780–83 and 1790–1813, in France. His *Letters from an*
American Farmer (1782) explores the social and political issues of the day,
including the horrors of slavery. He was quite critical of the harsh punishment of slaves in Charleston, South Carolina, comparing that region to New
York, where, he believed, slaves were better treated. Crèvecoeur's recollections illuminate the vast regional differences of the system long before the
rise of the cotton kingdom.

While all is joy, festivity, and happiness in Charles-Town, would you
imagine that scenes of misery overspread in the country? Their ears by
habit are become deaf, their hearts are hardened; they neither see, hear,
nor feel for the woes of their poor slaves, from whose painful labours all
their wealth proceeds. Here the horrors of slavery, the hardship of incessant
toils, are unseen; and no one thinks with compassion of those showers of
sweat and of tears which from the bodies of Africans, daily drop, and
moisten the ground they till. The cracks of the whip urging these miserable
beings to excessive labour, are far too distant from the gay Capital to be

Hector St. John Crèvecoeur, *Letters from an American Farmer* (London, T. Davies,
1782), pp. 155–60, 166–68.

heard. The chosen race eat, drink, and live happy, while the unfortunate
one grubs up the ground, raises indigo, or husks the rice; exposed to a sun
full as scorching as their native one; without the support of good food,
without the cordials of any cheering liquor. This great contrast has often
afforded me subjects of the most conflicting meditation. On the one side,
behold a people enjoying all that life affords most bewitching and pleasurable, without labour, without fatigue, hardly subjected to the trouble of
wishing. With gold, dug from Peruvian mountains, they order vessels to
the coasts of Guinea; by virtue of that gold, wars, murders, and devastations
are committed in some harmless, peaceable African neighbourhood, where
dwelt innocent people, who even knew not but that all men were black.
The daughter torn from her weeping mother, the child from the wretched
parents, the wife from the loving husband; whole families swept away and
brought through storms and tempests to this rich metropolis! There, arranged like horses at a fair, they are branded like cattle, and then driven to
toil, to starve, and to languish for a few years on the different plantations
of these citizens. And for whom must they work? For persons they know
not, and who have no other power over them than that of violence, no
other right than what this accursed metal has given them! Strange order of
things! Oh, Nature, where art thou?—Are not these blacks thy children as
well as we? On the other side, nothing is to be seen but the most diffusive
misery and wretchedness, unrelieved even in thought or wish! Day after day
they drudge on without any prospect of ever reaping for themselves; they
are obliged to devote their lives, their limbs, their will, and every vital exertion to swell the wealth of masters; who look not upon them with half
the kindness and affection with which they consider their dogs and horses.
Kindness and affection are not the portion of those who will till the earth,
who carry the burdens, who convert the logs into useful boards. This reward, simple and natural as one would conceive it, would border on humanity; and planters must have none of it!

If Negroes are permitted to become fathers, this fatal indulgence only
tends to increase their misery: the poor companions of their scanty pleasures
are likewise the companions of their labours; and when at some critical
season they could wish to see them relieved, with tears in their eyes they
behold them perhaps doubly oppressed, obliged to bear the burden of
nature—a fatal present—as well as that of unabated tasks. How many have
I seen cursing the irresistible propensity, and regretting, that by having
tasted of those harmless joys, they had become the authors of double
misery to their wives. Like their masters, they are not permitted to partake
of those ineffable sensations with which Nature inspires the hearts of
fathers and mothers; they must repel them all, and become callous and
passive. This unnatural state often occasions the most acute, the most

pungent of their afflictions; they have no time, like us, tenderly to rear
their helpless off-spring, to nurse them on their knees, to enjoy the delight
of being parents. Their paternal fondness is embittered by considering,
that if their children live, they must live to be slaves like themselves; no
time is allowed them to exercise their pious office, the mothers must
fasten them on their backs, and, with this double load, follow their hus-
bands in the fields, where they too often hear no other sound than that of
the voice or whip of the taskmaster, and the cries of their infants, broiling
in the sun. These unfortunate creatures cry and weep like their parents,
without a possibility of relief; the very instinct of the brute, so laudable,
so irresistible, runs counter here to their master's interest; and to that god,
all the laws of Nature must give way. Thus planters get rich; so raw, so
unexperienced am I in this mode of life, that were I to be possessed of a
plantation, and my slaves treated as in general they are here, never could
I rest in peace; my sleep would be perpetually disturbed by a retrospect
of the frauds committed in Africa, in order to entrap them; frauds surpass-
ing in enormity everything which a common mind can possibly conceive.
I should be thinking of the barbarous treatment they meet with on ship-
board; of their anguish, of the despair necessarily inspired by their situation, when torn from their friends and relations; when delivered into the
hands of a people differently coloured, whom they cannot understand;
carried in a strange machine over an ever agitated element, which they had
never seen before; and finally delivered over to the severities of the whip-
pers, and the excessive labours of the field. Can it be possible that the force
of custom should ever make me deaf to all these reflections, and as insensi-
ble to the injustice of that trade, and to their miseries, as the rich inhabitants
of this town seem to be? What then is man; this being who boasts so much
of the excellence and dignity of his nature, among that variety of inscru-
table mysteries, of unsolvable problems, with which he is surrounded? The
reason why man has been thus created, is not the least astonishing! It is
said, I know, that they are much happier here than in the West Indies; because land being cheaper upon this continent than in those islands, the
fields allowed them to raise their subsistence from, are in general more extensive. The only possible chance of any alleviation depends on the humour
of the planters, who, bred in the midst of slaves, learn from the example
of their parents to despise them; and seldom conceive either from religion
or philosophy, any ideas that tend to make their fate less calamitous; except some strong native tenderness of heart, some rays of philanthropy,
overcome the obduracy contracted by habit.

    I have not resided here long enough to become insensible of pain for
the objects which I every day behold. In the choice of my friends and acquaintance, I always endeavour to find out those whose dispositions are

somewhat congenial with my own. We have slaves likewise in our northern provinces; I hope the time draws near when they will be all emancipated; but how different their lot, how different their situation, in every possible respect! They enjoy as much liberty as their masters, they are as well clad, and as well fed; in health and sickness they are tenderly taken care of; they live under the same roof, and are, truly speaking, a part of our families. Many of them are taught to read and write, and are well instructed in the principles of religion; they are the companions of our labours, and treated as such; they enjoy many perquisites, many established holidays, and are not obliged to work more than white people. They marry where inclination leads them; visit their wives every week; are as decently clad as the common people; they are indulged in educating, cherishing, and chastising their children, who are taught subordination to them as their lawful parents: in short, they participate in many of the benefits of our society without being obliged to bear any of its burdens. They are fat, healthy, and hearty, and far from repining at their fate; they think themselves happier than many of the lower class whites: they share with their masters the wheat and meat provision they help to raise; many of those whom the good Quakers have emancipated have received that great benefit with tears of regret, and have never quitted, though free, their former masters and bene-factors.

But is it really true as I have heard it asserted here, that those blacks are incapable of feeling the spurs of emulation, and the cheerful sound of en-couragement? By no means; there are a thousand proofs existing of their gratitude and fidelity: those hearts in which such noble dispositions can grow, are then like ours; they are susceptible of every generous sentiment, of every useful motive of action; they are capable of receiving lights, of imbibing ideas that would greatly alleviate the weight of their miseries. But what methods have in general been made use of to obtain so desirable an end? None; the day in which they arrive and are sold, is the first of their labours; labours, which from that hour admit of no respite; for though in-dulged by law with relaxation on Sundays, they are obliged to employ that time which is intended for rest, to till their little plantations. What can be expected from wretches in such circumstances? Forced from their native country, cruelly treated when on board, and not less so on the plantations to which they are driven; is there anything in this treatment but what must kindle all the passions, sow the seeds of inveterate resentment, and nourish a wish of perpetual revenge? They are left to the irresistible effects of those strong and natural propensities; the blows they receive, are they conducive to extinguish them, or to win their affections? They are neither soothed by the hopes that their slavery will ever terminate but with their lives; or yet encouraged by the goodness of their food, or the mildness of their

treatment. The very hopes held out to mankind by religion, that consola-
tory system, so useful to the miserable, are never presented to them; neither
moral nor physical means are made use of to soften their chains; they are
left in their original and untutored state; that very state wherein the natural
propensities of revenge and warm passions are so soon kindled. Cheered
by no one single motive that can impel the will, or excite their efforts;
nothing but terrors and punishments are presented to them: death is denounced if they run away; horrid delaceration if they speak with their
native freedom; perpetually awed by the terrible cracks of whips, or by
the fear of capital punishments, while even those punishments often fail
of their purpose.

. . . .

The following scene will I hope account for these melancholy reflections,
and apologise for the gloomy thoughts with which I have filled this letter:
my mind is, and always has been, oppressed since I became a witness to it.
I was not long since invited to dine with a planter who lived three miles
from ———, where he then resided. In order to avoid the heat of the sun,
I resolved to go on foot, sheltered in a small path, leading through a pleasant
wood. I was leisurely travelling along, attentively examining some peculiar
plants which I had collected, when all at once I felt the air strongly agitated,
though the day was perfectly calm and sultry. I immediately cast my eyes
toward the cleared ground, from which I was but a small distance, in
order to see whether it was not occasioned by a sudden shower; when at
that instant a sound resembling a deep rough voice, uttered, as I thought,
a few inarticulate monosyllables. Alarmed and surprised, I precipitately
looked all round, when I perceived at about six rods distance something
resembling a cage, suspended to the limbs of a tree; all the branches of
which appeared covered with large birds of prey, fluttering about, and
anxiously endeavouring to perch on the cage. Actuated by an involuntary
motion of my hands, more than by any design of my mind, I fired at them;
they all flew to a short distance, with a most hideous noise: when, horrid
to think and painful to repeat, I perceived a Negro, suspended in the cage,
and left there to expire! I shudder when I recollect that the birds had already picked out his eyes, his cheek bones were bare; his arms had been
attacked in several places, and his body seemed covered with a multitude
of wounds. From the edges of the hollow sockets and from the lacerations
with which he was disfigured, the blood slowly dropped, and tinged the
ground beneath. No sooner were the birds flown, than swarms of insects
covered the whole body of this unfortunate wretch, eager to feed on his
mangled flesh and to drink his blood. I found myself suddenly arrested
by the power of affright and terror; my nerves were convulsed; I trembled,
I stood motionless, involuntarily contemplating the fate of this Negro, in

all its dismal latitude. The living spectre though deprived of his eyes, could still distinctly hear, and in his uncouth dialect begged me to give him some water to allay his thirst. Humanity herself would have recoiled back with horror; she would have balanced whether to lessen such reliefless distress, or mercifully with one blow to end this dreadful scene of agonising torture! Had I had a ball in my gun, I certainly should have despatched him; but finding myself unable to perform so kind an office, I sought, though trembling, to relieve him as well as I could. A shell ready fixed to a pole, which had been used by some Negroes, presented itself to me; I filled it with water, and with trembling hands I guided it to the quivering lips of the wretched sufferer. Urged by the irresistible power of thirst, he endeavoured to meet it, as he instinctively guessed its approach by the noise it made in passing through the bars of the cage. "Tankè, you white man, tankè you, putè somè poison and givè me." "How long have you been hanging there?" I asked him. "Two days, and me no die; the birds, the birds; aaah me!" Oppressed with the reflections which this shocking spectacle afforded me, I mustered strength enough to walk away, and soon reached the house at which I intended to dine. There I heard that the reason for this slave being thus punished, was on account of his having killed the overseer of the plantation. They told me that the laws of self-preservation rendered such executions necessary; and supported the doctrine of slavery with the arguments generally made use of to justify the practice; with the repetition of which I shall not trouble you at present.—Adieu.

6: SLAVE CODES IN THE EARLY REPUBLIC

*There have been several instances in America of
Negroes . . . changing their colour. . . .*

The Duc de la Rochefoucauld-Liancourt, François Alexandre Frédéric
(1747–1827), French philanthropist, humanitarian, and member of the
Estates-General, emigrated to the United States in 1794, remaining until
1798. Many subjects in the early republic interested the duke, including the
nature of laws and prison reform. Beginning in 1795 he toured the states
and Canada for three years, investigating social and legal conditions of blacks
and whites. Frédéric was disturbed and candid about the inequities of
Maryland's free black and slave codes.

I must not omit to mention a very great natural curiosity, that I saw on
my journey to Philadelphia—a Negro of Virginia, whose parents were both
Negroes; and who, gradually changing his native hue, became white. This
man continued black till he was forty years of age, when the skin of his
fingers, near the nails, began at first to assume a lighter colour, and con
tinued to grow lighter and lighter till it was perfectly white. The process
was the same in almost all the different parts of his body. His legs, thighs,
arms, and hands are white, with the exception of a few spots of different
sizes, which are brown, some of a deeper shade than others, but all being
lighter towards the edges. His neck and shoulders are of the same complex-

Duc de la Rochefoucauld-Liancourt, *Travels through the United States of North
America, the Country of the Iroquois, and Upper Canada, in the Years 1795, 1796,
and 1797* (London, R. Phillips, 1799), vol. 3, pp. 263–65, 553–56, 569–73.

ion as the skin of people with red hair; and is freckled in the same manner. Straight and smooth hair is partially substituted for his natural wool. On his breast there remain tufts of the wool; but they fall off daily, and are succeeded by black or grey hairs. His face is white from the hair to the lowest extremity of his forehead; his nose is black, the rest of his face a kind of brown, deepest towards the nose, and gradually growing light as it approaches the white part. His head, all of which is black, is still covered with wool. His private parts, he says, are less advanced in this progress, although the change is begun in them. By his own account, a sensible progress has been made in this metamorphosis of his person during the time he has been travelling, which has been for the last three months; and there is no doubt but in a short time he will become entirely white. He is, at present, one and forty years of age.

There is no reason to question the extraction of this Negro; he having served the whole of [the] last war in a corps of pioneers, and is besides well known in Virginia, where he has generally resided, and furnished with certificates sufficient to satisfy persons disposed to question the fact. The change has not been attended with any sickness. This man travels about the country to show himself for money. It is to be observed, that there have been several instances in America of Negroes, either mulattos or Indians, changing their colour; some after illness and others in a perfect state of health; but there is no instance of the change being as complete as this.

The laws respecting the Negroes are derived from an English institute of the year 1740. A justice of the peace, with three freemen of the neighbourhood, examine into, and decide upon, the crimes of Negroes. No defender is allowed to the poor wretch accused; and his judges have power to condemn him to whatever mode of death they shall think proper. Simple theft by a Negro is punished with death. When the crime is not such as to deserve capital punishment, a justice of the peace, with a single freeman, may, in this case, condemn to whatever lighter punishment they shall please to inflict. For the murder of a Negro with malicious intent, a white man pays a fine of three thousand six hundred and eighty dollars. If he have only beaten the Negro, without intention of murder, till his death ensued, the fine is but one thousand five hundred dollars. He who maims a Negro, puts out his eyes, cuts off his tongue, or castrates him, pays only a fine of four hundred and twenty-eight dollars. In all these cases, the white man is imprisoned till the fine be paid. It is easy to see, that a white man can, in such case, seldom be convicted; as Negroes are incapable by law of giving evidence; and no white man will readily offer his testimony in favour of a black, against a person of his own colour. A Negro slaying a white man, in the defence of his master, is pardoned. But, if he do the same thing, or even but wound a white man, in the defence of his own life, he will eventually be put to death. A more diligent examination of the laws might discover many other odious things in them.

The most enlightened people in Carolina see the necessity of an alteration of these laws; and it is said, that the meeting of a new legislature will take up this matter. I am afraid, that any reform will not be such as it ought to be. It should seem, that those who mention this subject are strongly impressed with the idea of the necessity of the measure.

House robberies are more frequent in Maryland; five or six trials for this offence occur almost every session. Murders are very rare. The judges attribute the multiplicity of robberies to the free Negroes, who are numerous in the state of Maryland: I have heard the same accusation preferred against them in all the states where slavery is permitted. Such a charge is consequently a strong argument with the slave-holders against the abolition of slavery; but the evil, if it exists, as I am led to believe it does, is still to be attributed to the state of slavery, in which these newly-freed men have been previously kept, and from which they have been emancipated without any preparation for a state of freedom.

It is natural to suppose, that a slave, harassed by continual labour, driven by the scourge to toil in the open fields whether he is healthy or sick, considers liberty merely as a release from labour. Whilst he was a slave, food of some sort or other was always provided for him, without the least care on his part; since he was aware that no industry, or attention of his, would procure him either better food or clothing. Labour therefore brought nothing but fatigue, and he became of course indolent and careless. The moments of his liberty are enjoyed in a cessation of toil; for the lash no longer resounds in his ears: he feels the wants of nature; no education has been bestowed on him but that of slavery, which teaches him to cheat, to steal, to lie; and he satisfies those wants, for which industry has not provided, by pilfering the corn or provisions of his neighbours, and becomes the receiver of goods stolen by the slaves.

Though such are the necessary consequences of freedom, thus bestowed upon a slave, they should by no means operate unfavourably with those who are desirous of the gradual emancipation of the Negroes; who conceive that by a careful and liberal preparation for such a benevolent measure, adapted to the number of Negroes in the country, and many other circumstances, the greater part of the evils described may be avoided, and may at length be entirely prevented, if not in the present, at least in the future generation. But how can we hope for so general a spirit of philanthropy among men who look only to their present interest, of which they imagine it destructive?

In the State of Maryland, slaves are tried in the same courts as whites;

they have also the privilege of trial by juries. The punishments for the blacks are very severe; but the manners of the people are mild, at least in that part of Maryland where I am at present, and prevail over the rigour of the laws. I was witness to a fact which proves the humanity of the judges, and their desire to render equal justice to the accused, whether whites or slaves. A female Negro is now in prison accused of having poisoned a child, and of having attempted to poison her mistress. Her mistress, who is her accuser, being a woman of considerable consequence in the country, and allied to a family of great influence in the county, the judges, jealous of the effects of that influence on the jury, have availed themselves of the power they possess of referring the trial to the general court of the district, which is held sixty miles from Chester, that the accused may enjoy every possible chance of a fair and impartial trial.

· ·

The population of white people in the east part of Maryland, diminishes instead of augmenting. In a country abounding in slaves, the whites do not apply much to labour. Their ambition consists in buying Negroes; they buy them with the first sum of money they get, and when they have two of them they leave off working themselves: this small number is not sufficient to keep their lands in good order according to the tillage of the country, bad as it may be. The small farmers among the whites thus leaving off labour augment their expenses, and their affairs are soon in a bad condition. These, and those who have never been able to purchase Negroes, find themselves in an inferior situation to their neighbours who have many slaves: displeased with their station, they soon think of establishing themselves in a country where land is cheaper, and where they shall not be so much surpassed by proprietors so disproportionably richer than themselves. So that all these small farms, the supporting of which becomes every year more chargeable, because the wood for making the fences for enclosure is more scarce, and hand-labour at a higher price, are put to sale, and are bought by rich planters, and those who have sold them go to establish themselves in Kentucky, in Tennessee, and in the countries of the West. By this the province does not gain in agricultural improvements what it loses in population; its lands are not better managed, their produce is not increased but often diminished, because the purchaser of them looks rather at a good foundation for his property, that is to say, a sure augmentation of property than an increase of revenue.

Here, as in other places, when the utility of Negro slaves to the interests of the master is closely examined, compared with the employment of every other kind of labour, it will be found that in reality it has none. The old men and women, children, and pregnant females, must be fed and clothed, and taken care of in sickness. Nothing is more common than to see the proprietor of eighty slaves unable to bring thirty to work in the field at the same time. Ten workmen, hired by the year, will perform at least as much labour as these thirty slaves, and the master has nothing to do but to pay them. There are already a great many masters aware of this calculation, and many perceive the inconvenience of slaves, who, as I have said, cause all the white labourers to quit the country who would apply themselves to work if there were no slaves. Masters are embarrassed with their Negroes, the population of whom would otherwise augment in the southern states in the same proportion as that of the whites in other parts of America; but while they all perceive the inconveniency of slavery, they are the first to oppose the measure of the legislature's making a law for the gradual abolition of slavery.

The proprietors of Negroes complain already that since their population has increased, they are less submissive and more turbulent than they were before. These symptoms ought to teach them the necessity of doing something speedily towards putting an end to this state of slavery, which will be sooner or later very dangerous to the masters; but they fall asleep over this as they do over other dangers; and in this case, as in all others, it is acknowledged that foresight is null and void among the people of America.

. . . .

In the township of St. Paul [South Carolina] a free Negro, who from his early youth carefully stored up the produce of his industry, possesses a plantation of two hundred slaves. Instances of this kind are not rare, I understand, in St. Domingo; but such a plantation is here a phenomenon. The severity excepted, with which this emancipated slave treats his Negroes, his conduct is said to be regular and good. His name is *Pindaim,* and he is eighty-five years old. He has married a white woman, and has given his daughter, a mulatto, to a white man.

SIR WILLIAM HOWARD RUSSELL

7: SLAVE AUCTION IN MONTGOMERY, ALABAMA

The more orderly, methodical, and perfect the
arrangements for economising slave labour are,
the more hateful and odious does slavery become.

From 1861 to 1865 hundreds of critical foreign war correspondents
were attracted to America desiring first-hand information on the Civil War.
Among them was an Irish journalist for the London *Times,* Sir William
Howard Russell (1820-1907). Russell's career included news assignments
during the Crimean War. But domestic affairs were as important to him as
military operations. During his sojourn in the United States, Russell spent
some time reporting on the daily lives of the slaves and their masters. He
was personally affronted by the hideous character of a Montgomery, Alabama,
slave auction and a sugar cane plantation in Louisiana in 1861.

The environs of Montgomery are agreeable—well-wooded, undulating,
villas abounding, public gardens, and a large Negro and mulatto suburb. It
is not usual, as far as I can judge, to see women riding on horseback in the
South, but on the road here we encountered several.

After breakfast I walked down with Senator Wigfall to the capitol of
Montgomery—one of the true Athenian Yankeeized structures of this novo-
classic land, erected on a site worthy of a better fate and edifice. By an
open cistern, on our way, I came on a gentleman engaged in disposing of
some living ebony carvings to a small circle, who had more curiosity than
cash, for they did not at all respond to the energetic appeals of the auctioneer

William H. Russell, *My Diary North and South,* vol. 1 (London, Bradbury and Evans,
1863), pp. 241-46, 391-92, 395-99.

The auctioneer, who was an ill-favoured, dissipated-looking rascal, had his "article" beside him on, not in a deal packing-case—a stout young Negro badly dressed and ill-shod, who stood with all his goods fastened in a small bundle in his hand, looking out at the small and listless gathering of men, who, whittling and chewing, had moved out from the shady side of the street as they saw the man put up. The chattel character of slavery in the States renders it most repulsive. What a pity the nigger is not polypoid— so that he could be cut up in junks, and each junk should reproduce itself!

A man in a cart, some volunteers in coarse uniforms, a few Irish labourers in a long van, and four or five men in the usual black coat, satin waistcoat, and black hat, constituted the audience, whom the auctioneer addressed volubly: "A prime field hand! Just look at him—good-natered, well tempered; no marks, nary sign of bad about him! En-i-ne hunthered—only nine hun-ther-ed and fifty dol'rs for 'em! Why, it's quite rad-aklous! Nine hundred and fifty dol'rs! I can't raly—That's good. Thank you, sir. Twenty-five bid— nine hun-therd and seventy-five dol'rs for this most useful hand." The price rose to one thousand dollars, at which the useful hand was knocked down to one of the black hats near me. The auctioneer and the Negro and his buyer all walked off together to settle the transaction, and the crowd moved away.

"That nigger went cheap," said one of them to a companion, as he walked towards the shade. "Yes, *Sirr!* Niggers is cheap now—that's a fact." I must admit that I felt myself indulging a sort of reflection whether it would not be nice to own a man as absolutely as one might possess a horse —to hold him subject to my will and pleasure, as if he were a brute beast without the power of kicking or biting—to make him work for me—to hold his fate in my hands: but the thought was for a moment. It was followed by disgust.

I have seen slave markets in the East, where the traditions of the race, the condition of family and social relations divest slavery of the most odious characteristics which pertain to it in the States; but the use of the English tongue in such a transaction, and the idea of its taking place among a civilised Christian people, produced in me a feeling of inexpressible loath-ing and indignation. Yesterday I was much struck by the intelligence, activ-ity, and desire to please of a good-looking coloured waiter, who seemed so light-hearted and light-coloured I could not imagine he was a slave. So one of our party, who was an American, asked him: "What are you, boy—a free nigger?" Of course he knew that in Alabama it was most unlikely he could reply in the affirmative. The young man's smile died away from his lips, a flush of blood embrowned the face for a moment, and he answered in a sad, low tone: "No, sir! I b'long to Massa Jackson," and left the room at once. As I stood at an upper window of the capitol, and looked on the wide expanse of richly wooded, well-cultivated land which sweeps round the hill side away to the horizon; I could not help thinking of the misery and cruelty which must have been borne in tilling the land and raising the houses and streets of the dominant race before whom one nationality of coloured people has perished within the memory of man. The misery and cruelty of the system are established by the advertisements for runaway Negroes, and by the description of the stigmata on their persons—whippings, and brandings, scars and cuts—though these, indeed, are less frequent here than in the border States.

. . . .

June 5th.—The smart Negro who waited on me this morning spoke English. I asked him if he knew how to read and write.—"We must not do that, sir." "Where were you born?"—"I were raised on the plantation, Massa, but I have been to New Orleens"; and then he added, with an air of pride, "I sp'ose, sir, Massa Burnside not take less than 1500 dollars for me." Downstairs to breakfast, the luxuries of which are fish, prawns, and red meat which has been sent for to Donaldsonville by [a] boat rowed by an old Negro. Breakfast over, I walked down to the yard, where the horses were waiting, and proceeded to visit the saccharine principality. Mr. Seal, the overseer of this portion of the estate, was my guide, if not philosopher and friend. Our road lay through a lane formed by a cart-track, between fields of Indian corn just beginning to flower—as it is called technically, to "tassel"—and sugar-cane. There were stalks of the former twelve or fifteen feet in height, with three or four ears each, round which the pea twined in leafy masses. The maize affords food to the Negro, and the husks are eaten by the horses and mules, which also fatten on the peas in rolling time.

The wealth of the land is inexhaustible: all the soil requires is an alternation of maize and cane; and the latter, when cut in the stalk, called "ratoons," at the end of the year, produces a fresh crop, yielding excellent sugar. The cane is grown from stalks which are laid in pits during the winter till the ground has been ploughed, when each piece of cane is laid longitudinally on the ridge and covered with earth, and from each joint of the stalk springs forth a separate sprout when the crop begins to grow. At present the sugar-cane is waiting for its full development, but the Negro labour around its stem has ceased. It is planted in long continuous furrows, and although the palm-like tops have not yet united in a uniform arch over the six feet which separates row from row, the stalks are higher than a man. The plantation is pierced with waggon roads, for the purpose of conveying the cane to the sugar-mills, and these again are intersected by and run parallel with drains and ditches, portions of the great system of irrigation and drainage, in connection with a canal to carry off the surplus water to a bayou. The extent of these works may be estimated by the fact that there are thirty miles of road and twenty miles of open deep drainage through the estate, and that the main canal is fifteen feet wide, and at present four feet deep; but in the midst of this waste of plenty and wealth, where are the human beings who produce both? One must go far to discover them; they are buried in sugar and in maize, or hidden in Negro quarters.

The first place I visited with the overseer was a new sugar-house, which Negro carpenters and masons were engaged in erecting. It would have been amusing had not the subject been so grave, to hear the overseer's praises of the intelligence and skill of these workmen, and his boast that they did all the work of skilled labourers on the estate, and then to listen to him, in a few minutes, expatiating on the utter helplessness and ignorance of the black race, their incapacity to do any good, or even to take care of themselves.

There are four sugar-houses on this portion of Mr. Burnside's estate, consisting of grinding-mills, boiling-houses, and crystallising sheds.

The sugar-house is the capital of the Negro quarters, and to each of them is attached an enclosure, in which there is a double row of single-storied wooden cottages, divided into two or four rooms. An avenue of trees runs down the centre of the Negro street, and behind each hut are rude poultry-hutches, which, with geese and turkeys and a few pigs, form the perquisites of the slaves, and the sole source from which they derive their acquaintance with currency. Their terms are strictly cash. An old Negro brought up some ducks to Mr. Burnside last night, and offered the lot of six for three dollars. "Very well, Louis; if you come to-morrow, I'll pay you." "No, massa; me want de money now." "But won't you give me credit, Louis? Don't you think I'll pay the three dollars?" "Oh, pay some day, massa, sure enough. Massa good to pay de tree dollar; but this nigger want money now to buy food and things for him leetle family. They will trust massa at Donaldsville, but they won't trust this nigger." I was told that a thrifty Negro will sometimes make ten or twelve pounds a year from his corn and poultry; but he can have no inducement to hoard; for whatever is his, as well as himself, belongs to his master.

Mr. Seal conducted me to a kind of forcing-house, where the young Negroes are kept in charge of certain old crones too old for work, whilst their parents are away in the cane and Indian corn. A host of children of both sexes were seated in the verandah of a large wooden shed, or playing around it, very happily and noisily. I was glad to see the boys and girls of nine, ten, and eleven years of age were at this season, at all events, exempted from the cruel fate which befalls poor children of their age in the mining and manufacturing districts of England. At the sight of the overseer the little ones came forward in tumultuous glee, babbling out, "Massa Seal," and evidently pleased to see him.

As a jolly agriculturist looks at his yearlings or young beeves, the kindly overseer, lolling in his saddle, pointed with his whip to the glistening fat ribs and corpulent paunches of his woolly-headed flock. "There's not a plantation in the State," quote he "can show such a lot of young niggers. The way to get them right is not to work the mothers too hard when they are near their time; to give them plenty to eat, and not to send them to the fields too soon." He told me the increase was about five per cent per annum. The children were quite sufficiently clad, ran about round us, patted the horses, felt our legs, tried to climb up on the stirrup, and twinkled their black and ochrey eyes at Massa Seal. Some were exceedingly fair; and Mr. Seal, observing that my eye followed these, murmured something about the overseers before Mr. Burnside's time being rather a bad lot. He talked about their colour and complexion quite openly; nor did it seem to strike him that there was any particular turpitude in the white man who had left his offspring as slaves on the plantation.

A tall, well-built lad of some nine or ten years stood by me, looking curiously into my face. "What is your name?" said I. "George," he replied. "Do you know how to read or write?" He evidently did not understand the question. "Do you go to church or chapel?" A dubious shake of the head. "Did you ever hear of our Saviour?" At this point Mr. Seal interposed, and said, "I think we had better go on, as the sun is getting hot," and so we rode gently through the little ones; and when we had got some distance he said, rather apologetically, "We don't think it right to put these things into their heads so young, it only disturbs their minds, and leads them astray."

Now, in this one quarter there were no less than eighty children, some twelve and some even fourteen years of age. No education—no God—their whole life—food and play, to strengthen their muscles and fit them for the work of a slave. "And when they die?" "Well," said Mr. Seal, "they are buried in that field there by their own people, and some of them have a sort of prayers over them, I believe." The overseer, it is certain, had no fastidious notions about slavery; it was to him the right thing in the right place, and his *summum bonum* was a high price for sugar, a good crop, and a healthy plantation. Nay, I am sure I would not wrong him if I said he could see no impropriety in running a good cargo of regular black slaves, who might clear the great backwood and swampy undergrowth, which was now exhausting the energies of his field-hands, in the absence of Irish navvies.

Each Negro gets 5 lbs. of pork a week, and as much Indian corn bread as he can eat, with a portion of molasses, and occasionally they have fish for breakfast. All the carpenters' and smiths' work, the erection of sheds, repairing of carts and ploughs, and the baking of bricks for the farm buildings, are done on the estate by the slaves. The machinery comes from the manufacturing cities of the North; but great efforts are made to procure it from New Orleans, where factories have been already established. On the borders of the forest the Negroes are allowed to plant corn for their own use, and sometimes they have an overplus, which they sell to their masters. Except when there is any harvest pressure on their hands, they have from noon on Saturday till dawn on Monday morning to do as they please, but they must not stir off the plantation on the road, unless with special permit, which is rarely granted.

There is an hospital on the estate, and even shrewd Mr. Seal did not perceive the conclusion that was to be drawn from his testimony to its excellent arrangements. "Once a nigger gets in there, he'd like to live there for the rest of his life." But are they not the happiest, most contented people in the world—at any rate, when they are in hospital? I declare that to me the more orderly, methodical, and perfect the arrangements for economising slave labour—regulating slaves—are, the more hateful and odious does slavery become.

III

QUASI-FREE BLACKS

*Even in the lowest house of ill-repute in the Free
States, no colored man is allowed to enter.*

Edward Dicey, 1862

The free black population in the United States in 1860 numbered
500,000, approximately one of every nine Afro-Americans. More than
half of them lived restricted lives in the slaveholding states, in some instances only one step removed from slavery. They dated back to the colonial era when bondsmen ran away or were manumitted by humanitarian
masters, by maternal status laws, as a reward for loyalty, or as a reward
for exposing slave conspiracies. Some were willed their freedom, and in
the North between 1783 and 1804 they were promised such in gradual
emancipation statutes.

The economic, social, and political lives of free blacks were in jeopardy
before and after the Revolution. Status varied around the country, depending upon black-white population ratios, white economic fluctuation, and
overall racial attitudes. Nationally, they had no federal rights, according
to the 1857 Dred Scott Supreme Court decision. Only after the Civil War
were they to receive recognition as citizens. States, however, had different
local practices, though none provided access to civil and judicial equality,
with the exception of the New England states where voting privileges were
granted. Their travels and residence in the antebellum South were limited
to counties and states of birth. The availability of jobs, property restrictions,
and planters' fears forced most to reside in and around the urban centers
of the Atlantic seaboard.

North and south, they acquired valuable employment skills and became
an integral factor in the economy. Ironically, black businesses, namely
funeral parlors, barber shops, and other self-help enterprises, thrived because of segregation. As a result, a small but important middle class developed in the cities. By 1860 New Orleans's free blacks owned $15,000,000

worth of property. By comparison, New York's blacks had total assets of $1,000,000. Money and time were spent less for future concerns than for immediate gratification in a society which limited their outlets to material consumption or fraternal and religious organization.

Most important of any pre–Civil War free black institutions was the church, which grew out of discrimination and the need for self-expression. The door was opened by Richard Allen, Absalom Jones, and their followers in 1787 when they split off from the white-run St. George's Methodist Episcopal Church of Philadelphia. By 1816 free Afro-Americans claimed independent Baptist congregations, the St. Thomas Protestant Episcopal Church, and the African Methodist order. They were not only houses of prayer. Education was provided as well as social and fund-raising affairs to accommodate the community's needs. Outspoken ministers and their followers were the backbone of the abolitionist and protest movement.

A small but growing literate population provided a market for the northern black press. The first newspaper, New York City's *Freedom's Journal* (1827–29), edited by John Russwurm and Samuel Cornish, was typical of the era's journals, presenting editorials on northern discrimination, white riots, and slavery, in addition to carrying news of the trends in the social life of urban blacks. Editors and preachers were among the first in the North to organize antislavery societies. The free black convention movement which originated in Philadelphia in 1830 symbolized their growing frustration. Some free black leaders put down the pen and picked up the torch. Denmark Vesey's unsuccessful effort to free slaves in South Carolina in 1822 was followed by David Walker, whose fiery 1829 *Appeal* denounced the society and called for slave rebellion. The fire burned on into the 1840s with similar cries by the Reverend Henry Highland Garnet.

Some free blacks chose the alternative of emigration as a solution to the problems of race. The back-to-Africa movement, beginning with Paul Cuffee's spirited move to Sierra Leone in 1811 and capped off by Martin Delany's short visit to West Africa in the late 1850s, was supported by nearly 15,000 blacks, many of whom eventually settled in the American Colonization Society's colony, Liberia. But Frederick Douglass, representative of most free blacks' interests, protested for a better life in America, not in Africa.

The Civil War presented an opportunity to change the conditions of free black and slave life. During the course of the bitter conflict, 180,000 black troops joined the Union side in search of the solution to racism and slavery. Forty-five thousand never returned home.

8: FREE BLACK SCHOOL IN THE NORTH

*The law, in truth, has left him in that most pitiable of
all conditions,* a masterless slave!

Thomas Hamilton

Thomas Hamilton (1789-1842), a Scottish professional soldier, retired
from army service in 1818 after an eight-year career to become a writer.
Hamilton visited the United States in November, 1830, and remained
until the summer of 1831, during which time he toured different states
to study American customs. The recollections of this trip, published as
Men and Manners in America (1833), reveal the author's disdain for the
imbalanced wealth, poverty, and lack of opportunity for the poor, white
and black. Hamilton was surprised about the position of "free" blacks and
the gulf between their educational goals and job opportunities. His visit
to a New York free black school in 1831 exposed the racial problem.

Having resolved to devote the day to the inspection of schools, I went
from that under the superintendence of Professor Griscomb, to another
for the education of children of colour. I here found about a hundred boys,
in whose countenances might be traced every possible gradation of complexion between those of the swarthy Ethiop and florid European. Indeed
several of the children were so fair, that I certainly never should have dis-
covered the lurking taint of African descent. In person they were clean
and neat, and though of course the offspring of the very lowest class of
the people, there was nothing in their dress or appearance indicative of ab-
ject poverty. The master struck me as an intelligent and benevolent man.

Thomas Hamilton, *Men and Manners in America* (London, T. Cadell, 1833), pp. 90-101.

He frankly answered all my questions, and evidently took pride in the proficiency of his pupils.

It has often happened to me, since my arrival in this country, to hear it gravely maintained by men of education and intelligence, that the Negroes were an inferior race, a link as it were between man and the brutes. Having enjoyed few opportunities of observation on people of colour in my own country, I was now glad to be enabled to enlarge my knowledge on a subject so interesting. I therefore requested the master to inform me whether the results of his experience had led to the inference, that the aptitude of the Negroe children for acquiring knowledge was inferior to that of the whites. In reply, he assured me they had not done so; and, on the contrary, declared, that in sagacity, perseverance, and capacity for the acquisition and retention of knowledge, his poor despised scholars were equal to any boys he had ever known. "But alas, sir!" said he, "to what end are these poor creatures taught acquirement, from the exercise of which they are destined to be debarred, by the prejudices of society? It is surely but a cruel mockery to cultivate talents, when in the present state of public feeling, there is no field open for their useful employment. Be his acquirements what they may, a Negroe is still a Negroe, or, in other words, a creature marked out for degradation, and exclusion from those objects which stimulate the hopes and powers of other men."

I observed, in reply, that I was not aware that, in those States in which slavery had been abolished, any such barrier existed as that to which he alluded. "In the State of New York, for instance," I asked, "are not all offices and professions open to the man of colour as well as to the white?"

"I see, sir," replied he, "that you are not a native of this country, or you would not have asked such a question." He then went on to inform me, that the exclusion in question did not arise from any legislative enactment, but from the tyranny of that prejudice, which, regarding the poor black as a being of inferior order, works its own fulfillment in making him so. There was no answering this, for it accorded too well with my own observations in society, not to carry my implicit belief.

The master then proceeded to explain the system of education adopted in the school, and subsequently afforded many gratifying proofs of the proficiency of his scholars. One class were employed in navigation, and worked several complicated problems with great accuracy and rapidity. A large proportion were perfectly conversant with arithmetic, and not a few with the lower mathematics. A long and rigid examination took place in geography, in the course of which questions were answered with facility, which I confess would have puzzled me exceedingly, had they been addressed to myself.

I had become so much interested in the little party-coloured crowd before me, that I recurred to our former discourse, and enquired of the master, what would probably become of his scholars on their being sent out into the world? Some trades, some description of labour of course were open to them, and I expressed my desire to know what these were. He told me they were few. The class studying navigation, were destined to be sailors; but let their talents be what they might, it was impossible they could rise to be officers of the paltriest merchantman that entered the waters of the United States. The office of cook or steward was indeed within the scope of their ambition; but it was just as feasible for the poor creatures to expect to become Chancellor of the State, as mate of a ship. In other pursuits it was the same. Some would become stonemasons, or bricklayers, and to the extent of carrying a hod, or handling a trowel, the course was clear before them; but the office of master-bricklayer was open to them in precisely the same sense as the Professorship of Natural Philosophy. No white artificer would serve under a coloured master. The most degraded Irish emigrant would scout the idea with indignation. As carpenters, shoemakers, or tailors, they were still arrested by the same barrier. In either of the latter capacities, indeed, they might work for people of their own complexion, but no *gentleman* would ever think of ordering garments of any sort from a *schneider* of cuticle less white than his own. Grocers they might be, but then who could conceive the possibility of a respectable household matron purchasing tea or spiceries from a vile "Nigger?" As barbers, they were more fortunate, and in that capacity might even enjoy the privilege of taking the President of the United States by the nose. Throughout the Union, the department of domestic service peculiarly belongs to them, though recently they are beginning to find rivals in the Irish emigrants, who come annually in swarms like locusts.

On the whole, I cannot help considering it a mistake to suppose, that slavery has been abolished in the Northern States of the Union. It is true, indeed, that in these States the power of compulsory labour no longer exists; and that one human being within their limits, can no longer claim property in the thews and sinews of another. But is this all that is implied in the boon of freedom? If the word mean any thing, it must mean the enjoyment of equal rights, and the unfettered exercise in each individual of such powers and faculties as God has given him. In this true meaning of the word, it may be safely asserted, that this poor degraded caste are still slaves. They are subjected to the most grinding and humiliating of all slaveries, that of universal and unconquerable prejudice. The whip, indeed, has been removed from the back of the Negro, but the chains are still on his limbs, and he bears the brand of degradation on his forehead. What is it but mere abuse of language to call him *free,* who is tyrannically deprived of all the motives to exertion which animate other men? The law, in truth, has left him in that most pitiable of all conditions, *a masterless slave.*

It cannot be denied, that the Negro population are still compelled, *as a class,* to be the hewers of wood, and drawers of water, to their fellow-citizens. *Citizens!* there is indeed something ludicrous in the application of the word to these miserable Pariahs. What privileges do they enjoy as such? Are they admissible upon a jury? Can they enroll themselves in the militia? Will a white man eat with them, or extend to them the hand of fellowship? Alas! if these men, so irresistibly manacled to degradation, are to be called *free,* tell us, at least, what stuff are slaves made of!

GUSTAVE de BEAUMONT

9: RACE RIOTS IN THE NORTH

*The true cause of hostility to the Negroes . . . was
the offended pride of the whites, at the pretensions
to equality shown by the colored people.*

On May 11, 1831, two French prison commissioners, leaving political
turmoil in their country, landed in the United States, beginning a nine
months official tour to study North American prison policy. Alexis de
Tocqueville and Gustave de Beaumont (1802–66) carried out their original
goals but both were more interested in the nature of American democracy.
De Tocqueville's published account, *Democracy in America* (1835), a discourse on United States institutions, became an immediate success. On the
other hand, Beaumont's *Marie,* a racial novel and sociological treatise appearing that same year, never gained the former's acclaim.

Marie focuses on the tragic love affair of a white man and a racially
mixed woman, and explores the dilemmas of race relations in the free states.
Beaumont's appendices to the novel are informative analyses of the modes
of racial conflict in the United States. The liberal Frenchman was especially
disturbed by northern antiabolitionist mob violence in 1834.

Gustave Auguste de Beaumont de La Bonninière, *Marie; or, Slavery in the United
States: A Novel of Jacksonian America,* translated by Barbara Chapman (Stanford
University Press, 1958), pp. 245–52 (Appendix L). Reprinted with the permission of
the publishers, Stanford University Press. Copyright © 1958 by the Board of Trustees
of the Leland Stanford Junior University.

RACE RIOTS IN THE NORTH

Intermarriages are certainly the best, if not the unique, means of fusing the white and the black races. They are also the most obvious index of equality. For this twofold reason, unions of this sort arouse the rancor of the Americans above all else.

Early in the year 1834 a minister of the Anti-Slavery Society, the Reverend Doctor Beriah Green, performed in Utica the marriage of a Negro to a young white girl, and there was a sort of popular uprising in the city, following which the reverend doctor was hanged in effigy on the public street.

Shortly afterward, Methodist and Presbyterian ministers in New York City married whites with colored people: this victory over prejudice encouraged the Negroes and roused the strong indignation of their enemies.

The month of July, 1834, arrived; the Americans celebrated the anniversary of their Declaration of Independence. For them this is always the occasion for long speeches on liberty and on the inalienable rights of man. The Negroes listened to some of these speeches, and their supporters did not omit on this occasion to remind them that the people of the black race have a liberty as sacred and rights as inviolable as the white men.

On July 7, an American, a friend to the Negroes, published in a newspaper a letter in which he announced that, in spite of a prejudice he scorned, he proposed to marry a young colored girl. That same day a meeting of colored people was held in Chatham Street Chapel and speeches were made, the texts of which were the equality of whites and Negroes and the abolition of slavery in the entire Union. By an unfortunate coincidence, the members of the church music society, who customarily met in the same place, wished to occupy it at the same time the African gathering was in progress. Thence arose a regrettable conflict which was quickly over, but it added still more to the irritation of the two groups. At the same time a pamphlet against slavery was being circulated, at the head of the pamphlet there was a little engraving of a slave dealer tearing a slave from the arms of his wife and children and driving him away with blows of a whip: nothing was neglected which might arouse the indignation of the Negroes and the zeal of their friends. Another meeting in Chatham Street Chapel was announced for the following day, July 9; the whites who sided with the Negroes promised to attend.

Then a very sharp feeling of annoyance became manifest in public opinion. The press showed itself unanimously hostile toward the colored people and bitterly derided the whites who so far forgot their dignity as to associate with wretched Negroes. The papers called the Negroes "the colored gentlemen," and the Negresses "the ladies of color"; they heaped sarcasm upon the white philanthropist who had published his intention to marry a colored woman. While the plans for the Chatham Street Chapel meeting were in progress, a powerful opposition was organized, and there was every indication that an unpleasant encounter would take place on that occasion. It is to be noted that at the time when these events took place the heat was excessive in New York. The 9th, 10th, and 11th of July were, in America, the hottest days in the year 1834. The temperature is not unconnected with popular agitations. On the appointed day (July 9), a great crowd surrounded Chatham Street Chapel; but the police, foreseeing a clash, had called off the meeting, which did not take place. However, in the crowd there was a certain number of people who had been drawn there solely in the hope of a fight, and who could not bear to go away without having done some mischief. It was the theater hour; they found out at that moment that at the Bowery Theater there was an English actor, named Farren, who was accused of having spoken ill of the American people. "To the Bowery! To the Bowery!" cried several voices; soon the crowd surged toward the theater, which, a moment later, presented a scene of nothing but trouble and confusion. When this deed had been accomplished, the agitators turned their minds again to the idea which had set them in motion.

Among the most zealous of the friends of the Negroes was an American named Arthur Tappan. They knew that he received colored people in his house, and he had even dared sometimes to appear in public in their company. A voice shouted, "To Tappan's house!" and the crowd immediately rushed there. The factionists smashed the windows, burst in the doors, and, finding no one at home, took the furniture, threw it into the street, and set it afire. The police arrived meanwhile; a struggle followed, in which the people were by turns the winners and the losers; at two in the morning the fighting stopped: so passed the day of the 9th. The next day the rebellion took on a still more serious character. It was found that the people planned to destroy Arthur Tappan's shops on Pearl Street and to attack the home of Dr. Cox, a Presbyterian minister devoted to the Negroes and their cause. Indeed, on the evening of the 10th, the crowd swept down on Dr. Cox's church, hurled missiles at its windows and doors, and withdrew. From there they went to the minister's house; but Dr. Cox and his family had left New York, having been warned of the danger that threatened them. Then the factionists began to demolish the house and were already at work when a detachment of the militia arrived, sent by the authorities; the insurgents, entrenched behind barricades made of overturned carts and wagons, put up a resistance. But after a half-hearted struggle, they yielded. On the same day, another church, belonging to the colored people and situated in the neighborhood of Laight Street, had been the object of the same attacks and outrages. The insurgents had tried to demolish it; a huge crowd had also gathered near Chatham Street Chapel, but dispersed peacefully upon the assurances of the proprietors of that edifice that they would never allow meetings to be held there having the abolition of slavery as their object. At midnight order was restored; but graver trouble was brewing for the next day, July 11.

It would seem certain that if, on the 10th and 11th, the authorities had taken energetic measures, the seditious movement would have had no consequences. It would have been enough to order the militia to meet force with force and use all their weapons against the insurgents, without any exceptions.

However, the group which demanded these energetic reprisals was not the strongest or most numerous. If the riots had been of a purely political nature, the majority would have been sure to arm itself immediately with all its powers and to crush the attacks or the resistance of the minority. But on this occasion the New Yorkers were divided between two opposed ideas. On the one hand, their respect for the law and their desire for peace and order made them feel the necessity of stopping the insurrection. On the other hand, the fate of the victims did not excite their interest at all. Indeed, the majority sympathized at heart with the violent actions of the lesser number; nevertheless, respect for principle, and even a sense of shame forced them to oppose these actions. This strange situation explains the slackness of the measures taken by the authorities against the insurrection.

From early morning on the 11th, numerous detachments of the militia were marched about; but it was known that they had received no order to fire on the people in case of renewed unrest. It was not, as has been said, the absence of the governor which made the use of firearms against the rioters impossible. The mayor of New York had the incontestable right to order this action; but he did not believe he should do so.

The first violence committed by the rioters was upon Arthur Tappan's shops. They flung a hail of stones through the windows of the building and were preparing more serious assaults when the arrival of the militia made them take to their heels. Toward nine in the evening, Dr. Cox's church, which had been attacked the day before, was assailed again by a furious mob; a thousand missiles were hurled against its walls; the police arrived but were repulsed by the people. At the same time, another group of rioters was giving free rein to more criminal and impious violence. In Spring Street,

the church of Dr. Ludlow was invaded. (The doctor's devotion to the cause
of the Negroes invited the hatred of the factionists.) Windows were broken,
doors smashed in, walls demolished; the ruins and fragments of the church
served as a barricade behind which the rebels took up their position; a serious engagement took place between the people and the militia; the alarm
was rung, the whole city was aroused; after several successes and reverses
on either side the victory rested with the militia. The insurgents withdrew,
but only to try more destruction elsewhere; they went to Dr. Ludlow's
house, broke the doors and windows, and committed all sorts of violence.
At the same time a church belonging to the blacks, and situated on Center
Street, gave way to the popular frenzy. The rumor had got about that a
few days before, the minister of this church, the Reverend Peter Williams,
as much to be respected for his virtues as for his religious spirit, had married
a colored man to a white woman. Thenceforward the fury of the crowd
grew to its full measure. The doors and windows were torn out, smashed,
demolished, to the accompaniment of cheers from the onlookers; everything they could find inside the church was seized and thrown into the
street. Soon the adjacent houses, occupied by colored people, were attacked
and broken into; the furniture was sacked, pillaged, and burned; the same
acts of violence were repeated in several other parts of the city. Other
churches were profaned; all property belonging to colored people was
declared outside the law. Their persons were respected no more than their
property; wherever a colored man appeared he was immediately attacked.
However, as all were terror-stricken, they hid themselves. Then the populace,
ingenious in its senseless fury, demanded that all the inhabitants should
light up their houses. They were thus forced to show themselves. Obeying
the commands of the people, a Negress appeared in the window after illu-
minating her house. A hail of stones fell upon her. Several colored families,
fearing the same fate, kept their windows dark, but the people, concluding
from this that Negroes were there, attacked and destroyed their houses.

It is only fair to say that in the face of this impious vandalism the immense majority of Americans, and even those who had sympathized the
day before with the vandals, were struck with disgust and horror. All those
in the city who had property to protect experienced a feeling of fright.
There was a general spirit of reaction, not in favor of the Negroes, but
against their oppressors. Everyone realized the danger of allowing a factional
and sacrilegious populace to continue longer in control of the city. It was
known that the insurgents intended to continue on the following day their
acts of violence and to destroy from top to bottom the churches and public
schools of the blacks. The mayor of the city gave the strictest orders to
the militia. The press addressed pitiless words to the rebels. Those who
showed the least tendency to sedition should be killed "like dogs," said

one paper on July 11 (*The Evening Post*). The militia marched, full of zeal, against the insurgents. Forthwith the sedition was put down for good. The mayor of the city gave an account of his actions to the City Council. He declared that up to the last day of the disturbance he had judged sufficient to repress it the means which events had proved were inefficacious; this naïve admission of an error whose consequences had been so deplorable seemed quite satisfactory. The mayor had merely followed the shifts of public opinion. When the rebellion broke out, it was fondly hoped that rigorous measures were not necessary to combat it; it affected only the colored people. They clung to that hope as long as possible. Everybody was grateful to the magistrates for having shared the common illusion.

The struggle being ended, each party tried to evade the responsibility for it. The majority of the population had risen up to repress the factionists: at the moment when the rebellion took on a character alarming to the city, the greater number attempted to lay the blame for the riots and their consequences on the victims. The insurgents were undoubtedly at fault for placing themselves above the law, but had not the Negroes and their supporters provoked them? One paper went so far as to demand that Mr. Tappan and Dr. Cox, whose ruin was caused by the riots, be accused of disturbing the public peace.

Those whose feelings were not so severe against the supporters of the blacks were at least indulgent toward their enemies. The press admirably seconded this tendency and furnished arguments to those whose reactions had been merely emotional.

The true cause of hostility against the Negroes, as I have said before, was the offended pride of the whites, at the pretensions to equality shown by the colored people. Now, a feeling of pride does not justify hatred and revenge. The Americans could not say: "We have allowed the Negroes to be attacked in our cities; we have allowed their private homes to be invaded, their churches to be profaned and torn down, because they had the audacity to wish to be our equals." This language, which would have been the truth, would have shown too much cynicism.

This is how the press helped the Americans out of their embarrassment: The advocates of the Negroes, it said, who wanted colored people to be the equals of the whites, demand the abolition of slavery in the whole Union; now, this is asking something contrary to the Constitution of the United States; in fact, the Constitution guarantees to the slave states the preservation of slavery as long as it pleases them to keep it; the interests of the North and the South are distinct. Those of the South rest on slavery. If the North works to destroy slavery in the South, it is doing a thing which is hostile and contrary to the very union of the states. Therefore, to favor the emancipation of the Negroes is to be an enemy of the Union.

The natural conclusion of this reasoning is that every good citizen in the United States should keep the blacks in servitude, and that the real enemies of the country are those who oppose slavery. The factionists who abandoned themselves for three days to the most iniquitous and impious violence were, fundamentally, animated by noble sentiments, while those who by their philanthropy toward an unhappy race had excited the just indignation of the whites were traitors to their country. Such are the consequences of a sophism.

Doubtless the Southern states could abolish slavery themselves; but since when have the Americans of the North lost the right to call attention to the evil of a vicious law? They destroyed slavery among themselves; and they are forbidden to wish for its destruction among their neighbors! They are not making a law, they are expressing a wish; if this wish is criminal, what becomes of the right of discussion, of freedom of speech and expression? Will this right cease to exist because it is used to attack the most monstrous of institutions? The Americans allow the vilest pamphleteer to write publicly that their President is a wretch, a swindler, an assassin; and an honorable man, moved by a profound conviction, cannot tell his fellow citizens that it is sad to see a whole race of men condemned to servitude; that nature revolts on seeing the child torn from its mother's breast, the husband separated from the wife, man beaten by man, and all in the name of the law! Finally, because there are still slaves in the South, must the freed Negroes be crushed without pity who, in New York, aspire to the rights of free men?

On July 12, the day after the insurrection, the Anti-Slavery Society published the following declaration:

1. We entirely disclaim any desire to promote or encourage intermarriage between white and colored persons.

2. We disclaim, and entirely disapprove, the language of a handbill recently circulated in this city, the tendency of which is thought to be to excite resistance to the Laws. Our principle is, that even hard laws are to be submitted to by all men, until they can by peaceable means be altered.

3. We disclaim, as we have always done, any intention to dissolve the Union, or to violate the Constitution and Laws of the country; or to ask of Congress any act transcending their constitutional powers; which the abolition of slavery by Congress, in any State, would do.

All this proves that in the United States, under the rule of popular sovereignty, there is a majority whose actions are irresistible, which crushes, breaks, annihilates everything which opposes its power and impedes its passions.

The events which have just been related roused a lamentable echo a few days later in the city of Philadelphia. On August 11, 1834, without cause or pretext, the whites attacked the Negroes; a sharp conflict ensued which lasted half a day. The agents of authority displayed a great energy against the rebellion, which was put down; but it threw the black population into a state of dejection. Two days later one of the papers reported that during the two days just past, steamboats going from Philadelphia to New Jersey had not ceased carrying a great quantity of colored people who, fearing for their lives in that city, determined to seek refuge elsewhere. Tents could be seen on the New Jersey shore, where the Negroes found temporary shelter while waiting to hire themselves out in a place where their lives and liberty would be assured.

Thus the Negroes, freed by the North, are forced back by tyranny into the Southern states, and find refuge only in the midst of slavery.

FRANCIS LIEBER

10: PRISON LIFE

*As to moral differences between the prisoners. . . , it
is a curious fact that in general the coloured people
behave themselves better; they are more orderly,
follow the laws more willingly, and work more steadily.*

Francis Lieber (1800-72), a German educator, fled to England and
then to the United States in 1827 after spending prison time in his country
for subversive radical activities. Lieber, a specialist in military law, politics,
and government, taught at South Carolina College (1835-56) and New
York's Columbia University (1857-72). He published numerous books,
including *Encyclopedia America.* During his stay in Boston, 1827-34,
Lieber traveled and studied American "peculiarities." The race question
interested him, and he spent time investigating black prison life in the
New York State Penitentiary (Sing Sing) in the early 1830s. Lieber, a
white supremacist, was surprised by the cleanliness of black inmates.
Nevertheless, after a tour of the South before 1835, he maintained that
black "physical odor" was a primary reason for the race's social segregation.

In the abstract, I hold slavery to be—philosophically, an absurdity (man
cannot become property)—morally a bane both to the slave and his owner
—historically, a direct violation of the spirit of the times we live in; and
with regard to public economy, a great malady to any society at all advanced in industry. I neither allow with Achille Murat, son to the late King
of Naples, that slavery is for the present condition of our southern states,
a highly desirable state of things, and conducive to the greatest advantage

Francis Lieber, *The Stranger in America: Comprising Sketches of the Manners,
Society and National Peculiarities of the United States, in a series of letters to a
friend in Europe* (London, R. Bentley, 1835), vol. 2, pp. 189–204.

of society (he does not speak of pecuniary advantages), nor do I at all agree with Duden, a German author, who, in his Report on a Journey to the Western States of the North American Union, in 1824 to 1827, inclusive—a work which contains some very valuable information, whenever the author abstains from political and historical disquisitions—supposes him self to have very nicely demonstrated, that a society has a full right to declare on what conditions it will admit other people, and how it will treat them in future, to make them incapable of participating in government, if the original society think fit to dictate in what relation of dependence they are to be placed, who, in short, sees no objection on the ground of justice to slavery, and altogether forgets that the idea of right between men, cannot, by any possibility, be established, except on the idea of mutual duties and obligations. He has recourse, in order to make out his case, to the relation of a father of a family to his children, as nearly every one does, who wishes to make out of a state of things founded on force, a state founded on reason, always forgetting that hardly two things in the world can be more different than family and state; the one based on instinct, love and forbearance, the other on justice, law, and right; the one to the end of the preservation of the species; which we have partly in common with the animals, the other in no degree whatever. Thrice unhappy comparison, entailed on us from ages when every thing in politics was poorly defined; whic has served the legitimatist and slave-dealer, the absolutist and the ambitious priest, as a cloak for sordid plans!

Whether the African race ever will have among them a Shakspeare, a Charlemagne, or Aristotle, I know not; nor is it necessary to know this, in order to settle the question as to their political capacity for participating in all civil rights and duties. There are many respectable coloured persons with us, and I believe none will conscientiously deny that, when fairly educated, they stand on quite as high a level of mental development as the lowest of the whites, who are nevertheless admitted to a full participation in all political privileges; nor that the question under consideration would ever have been started, did the African race not differ from ourselves in colour. One way of testing the comparative capability of the two classes, is to try coloured and white servants.

State prisons, where a large number of coloured and white people are kept under the close observance of intelligent men, and have to obey the same laws, to perform the same duties, and live upon the same diet, seemed to me to afford a peculiarly favourable opportunity of ascertaining certain facts relating to this subject. There are, of about eight hundred convicts in the penitentiary at Singsing, about two hundred individuals of colour. The physician of the prison, from whom I obtained my information, had not found that there was any striking difference between the diseases of the blacks and the whites, nor did they assume any different character in their course. I have been assured of the same by experienced physicians in large cities. However, as the coloured people resort to quacks, perhaps even more than the whites of the poorer classes, and have sometimes physicians of their own colour, closer examination would be still required to state any thing definite on this point.

It is for ever to be regretted that Doctor Spurzheim died so early. This able anatomist and observer of the configuration of the head, told me that one of the chief subjects of inquiry which he had laid out to himself in coming to this country, was to investigate the physical difference between the two races, and to settle something definite on this point. He intended to proceed to our southern states, and to make as many observations as possible on living and dead subjects. I trust that some able anatomist will take up the subject. It is a field where a fair name is yet to be won, and the consequences of a thorough inquiry into the minutest details of this subject might be of incalculable effect.

As to moral difference between the prisoners of the two colours in the above-mentioned penitentiary, it is a curious fact that in general the coloured people behave themselves better; they are more orderly, follow the laws more willingly, and work more steadily. The superintendent of that state-prison, a gentleman of much intelligence, and who bestowed unwearied attention to my often-repeated and troublesome inquiries both in person and by letter, did not attempt to explain the fact, he merely stated it as such, and as such I give it. Whatever reasons may be given for it, it deserves our attention. At one time, when I was walking with him through the building and we had entered one of the cells, after having given me some information on certain points of its architecture, he looked round and said, "I am sure this cell belongs to a coloured man." "Why so?" said I. "Because every thing looks neater, better arranged." On inquiry, we found that his surmise was correct. I was greatly surprised, and he then told me, that a coloured prisoner will generally keep his cell in more snug order than a white man. Equally interesting is the fact, that more coloured people ask for admission to the Sunday-school of the prison, and for instruction in reading, than white people; speaking merely of the proportion of individuals of both colours, who had no knowledge of reading.

Suppose, for argument's sake, that all the slave owners would be induced to emancipate their slaves to-day; or that the non-slave-holding states were willing to pay annually a large sum by way of compensation to the slave-holders, and that gradual emancipation could be thus effected. What would be the consequence? We should have a large increase of free coloured population, which, if we choose, might be politically as free as any class of our citizens. What would be gained? Political equality is of very little value compared to social equality. A race, socially degraded, or let us not call it degraded, one excluded from general society, and consequently from the broad course of civilization, is in a state of real suffering, and will necessarily generate in its bosom all kinds of vices and crimes. History affords us many instances to this effect. It is of no use whatever to be, in the eye of the law, equal to all others, if you are socially disabled, except you hope to attain social disfranchisement by means of the former. The free coloured race, the existence of which the argument supposes is large in number, would then remain an oppressed and degraded race, as long as they were not socially emancipated. Hence would arise, in order to obtain a real state of freedom for the emancipated slave, the necessity of amalgamation; by which I mean social intercourse as well as intermarriage: the latter would indeed be soon the consequence of the former. Two different races, equally free, and equally elevated in the social scale, hence equally cultivated and yet distinctly separated, cannot be imagined. Whoever does it, has other views of mankind, and learnt other lessons from history than myself. Whether this be founded upon prejudice or not, is not here the question; the prejudice is at any rate so founded in human nature that it would not depend upon us to change its effects.

Colour is something which strikes that sense which carries the most vivid impressions to the mind; you cannot expect the millions to disregard it; it presents too glaring an appearance; it is so striking an outward sign, that the idea of a well-marked difference between the two races cannot be well eradicated. I can very well imagine that in some cases a white man might lose his sensibility to this difference; in fact, I know a mulatto-man who is clerk with a bookseller, and I went often there and transacted business with him, without thinking of his colour. Generally, however, you cannot expect to find this indifference; especially, as another sense is affected by near intercourse with the coloured population. A peculiar odour is continually emanating, more especially in a warm climate, from the bodies of Negroes, even when cleanly, which renders them personally unpleasant to white people. There are individuals of the white race from whom a strong musky odour is emitted, unpleasant enough, it is true, and sometimes disgustingly repulsive; but that of a Negro is different. It resembles that exuding from the snake and beetle.

Soon after I arrived in this country, I found that this peculiar odour was considered one of the chief causes which would for ever prevent a social equalization of the two races, and I was anxious to ascertain for myself whether it had a real existence. I have very sensitive olfactory nerves, having received them from nature well organized, and have exercised them by studying botany, on my travels, &c. I have been able, on my pedestrian journeys, to scent a lake or a village at the distance of several miles, if the

wind was at all favourable; and yet I could not at first discover any difference between the odour of the Negroes and that I have often perceived
when many soldiers, after a long march, were assembled in the same room.
I was at that time in Boston; the summer was very cool, and no coloured
servant was in the house. Since I have gone farther south I must testify
to the correctness of the current statement. There are some very few who
deny this; so I knew an old lady who actually loved the music of quarrelling
or plaintively squalling cats. It was no affectation with her, of that I feel
convinced; yet I should not be willing to charge all the rest of mankind
with affectation or disregard to truth, because they declare that this kind
of music does not affect them with pleasurable sensations. Some nations
seem to be more affected by the scent of the African race than others, and
none more so than the English; Spaniards care less for it. Bolivar had some
coloured aides, if I am rightly informed; and in Brazil you may see black
priests administer the communion to white people. Yet even there is no
social mixture, no true social disfranchisement of the coloured.

In judging of this subject, it ought never to be forgotten that the stability
of social intercourse does not depend upon the agreement of a few broad
general ideas, but chiefly on an agreement upon the minor affairs of taste,
views, opinions, &c. I do not pretend to say that the white race is hand-
somer than the coloured; I can very well imagine that people, unaccustomed
to our faces, perceive in them, when they first become acquainted with our
race, all those shades of yellow, blue, and green, which the painter has to
mix with his colours to arrive at the true tints. Analyze a bloated face, and
you will shudder at all the ugliness it contains. Yet be this as it may, it is
clear that our views of beauty must essentially differ; and races who cannot,
in general, please each other, will never cement.

This strong barrier will for ever prevent a free social intercourse between
the two races. But, suppose it did not, shall a white man wish for a mixture
of them?—for, with me, a free social intercourse and intermarriage are one
and the same; one must lead to the other. If the love of country has ever
had any meaning attached to it, the love of race has a weightier meaning
still. I am a white man, and I for one love my race; that race which—however many misdeeds and crimes it may have forced history to enter on her
records, however often it may have suffered avarice to guide its actions and
blast the noblest plans, and however much its superior skill and knowledge
may have led it to superior and shameful incongruities—is, nevertheless,
the favoured one from which the Europeans have descended; who, with
their children, in other parts of the world, have risen to an immense intellectual superiority above all other tribes and nations. I for one do execrate
the idea of seeing this noble race degenerate into a yellow mongrel breed,
such as exists in Brazil and the Portuguese islands along the coast of Africa.

I for one pray that Heaven's best blessings, the extension of knowledge and civilization, may be showered down on our brethren of a darker skin, but desire with anxiety that the white race be continued in its purity— that race, which becomes master wherever it appears, because it unites in itself many good properties which are but scattered among other races— intelligence, sociability, activity, desire of private property, and elevation of mind.

IV

POSTBELLUM AGRARIAN LIFE

*If he were other than himself he would be a fit object
for compassion; But he is of too low a type to be unhappy, and is probably the only man who laughs
today in America.*

Lepel Henry Griffin, 1884

Congressional legislation abolishing slavery in 1865 destroyed the racial
order of southern whites accustomed to the tradition of black bondage. The
labor force that had been the bulwark of the plantation economy was now
freed of the chains and left to adapt to the ways of a free society. The ini-
tial reaction of the Johnson-backed southern governments was the establishment of black codes (except in North Carolina) which legitimized
pseudoslavery policies, binding ex-slaves to whites as apprentices in the
most exploitative contractual "agreements" imaginable. By 1867, Republican dominance wiped out the provisional governments, thereby eliminating
the codes. Laws, however, were a minor aspect of the racial situation. Racism was impossible to eradicate totally.

The overall southern labor situation guaranteed blacks an inferior position. Although the growth of industry in the South resulted in part from
the nature of the Civil War, its expansion as a major job provider did not
occur until the late nineteenth and early twentieth century. Even then
blacks remained fundamentally agricultural workers. The majority of
white immigrant workers flocked to the urban centers of the North and
Midwest, attracted to the available unskilled and semiskilled positions in
industry. White landowners did not want blacks to leave the South in
search of other opportunities. Blacks were in many ways "persuaded" to
remain in the fields, as supposedly free laborers. Questions of agricultural
stability and white hegemony were answered with the introduction of
sharecropping, tenant farming, debtor peonage, and convict leasing. Black
landownership existed, but on a relatively small scale. The majority of
blacks, on the other hand, now ex-slaves, in need of room, board, and
clothing, complied with the offerings. Some remained on the same planta-

tions of their slavery days; others migrated throughout the South, in search of their relatives and friends. Some were fortunate enough to homestead in the new states and territories of the West in the 1880s and 1890s.

The typical rural black family in the South eventually wound up in debt and despair. Sharecroppers and tenant farmers worked a plot of land for either part payment in crops or, in the case of tenancy, all the crops, after payment of a rental fee. Of course, the percentage of crops and rental fees varied throughout the nation in accordance with seasonal changes, crops, markets, landlords, and numerous other variables. Preseason debts mounted because of the leasing of tools, the hiring of plow animals, and the purchase of foodstuffs from the local merchant or landowner. Bad weather, death of the plow animals, tool breakage, and a conniving landlord contributed to the seemingly endless debt of the black family. Landlords preempted the better percentage of sharecroppers' labors, and for the tenant farmer the problem of crop sale was compounded by a market controlled by whites, rich and poor. The logic of survival dictated black compliance.

Black farmers joined together in the 1880s to form the Colored Farmers' Alliance. But even with one million members the organization could not exert enough force on the market to protect the rural blacks. Racial restrictions and violence in the jim-crow era posed a problem for any mass black movement. Jails were opened to the race as another mode of control, to be used as a source of labor in the form of convict leasing to those whites willing to pay local prison officials cheap fees. For rural blacks there was little hope but to escape to the city.

SIR GEORGE CAMPBELL

11: PROGRESS OF THE BLACK RACE

The white serfs of European countries took hundreds
of years to rise to the level which these Negroes have
attained in a dozen.

Born in Scotland, Sir George Campbell (1824–92) spent most of his
life in the service of England. Among other positions, he held that of mag-
istrate in India. While a member of the British Parliament (1875–92), Campbell took time off to visit the United States in the fall of 1878 to study
racial conditions in the post-Reconstruction South. Campbell, a prolific
author, was historically sympathetic to the native peoples he studied: Chinese, Irish, and Indians. His American study focuses on the effects of emancipation and the progress of the Afro-American. The work is generally
sympathetic to the race's educational, religious, and political desires but
concludes that blacks were the perfect laborers. Campbell believed that
major weaknesses existed in their families.

In the course of my tour I have had opportunities of conversing with
many men of many classes (and quite as much on one side of politics as
the other), who have had the greatest experience of the blacks in various
aspects—educational, industrial, political, and other. I am indebted to them
for information given to me with a freedom, frankness, and liberality for
which I cannot be sufficiently grateful; to none more so than to many
Southern gentlemen who have gone through all the bitternesses of a great
war on the losing side and the social revolution which followed—men whose

Sir George Campbell, *White and Black: The Outcome of a Visit to the United States*
(New York, R. Worthington, 1879), pp. 126–40.

good temper and fairness of statement, after all that has passed, commanded my admiration. I have visited not only the towns but the rural districts of four of the principal States formerly slave-holding, viz., Virginia, North Carolina, South Carolina, and Georgia; and it so happened that I was in South Carolina (the *ne plus ultra* of Southernism) on the day of the late general election. I have seen and conversed with the Negroes in their homes and in their fields, in factories, in churches, and in political meetings, and I think I have also been able to learn something of a very prominent part of the population—the Negresses.

THE CHARACTER AND CAPACITY OF THE NEGRO

The first and most difficult question is the capacity of the Negro as compared with other races. In one sense all men are born equal before God; but no one supposes that the capacities of all men are equal, or that the capacities of all races are equal, any more than the capacities of all breeds of cattle or dogs, which we know differ widely. There is, therefore, no *prima facie* improbability of a difference of capacity between the white Aryan and the Negro race, though I believe there is no ground for presuming that white races *must be* better than black.

It is unnecessary to try to distinguish between differences due to unassisted nature and those due to domestication and education. No doubt the varieties of wild animals found in different countries differ considerably; but the differences due to cultivation seem to be still more prominent in the animals and plants with which we are best acquainted. It is enough to take the Negro as he is, and his history and surroundings need only be briefly glanced at in so far as they afford some key to his present position and immediate prospects.

The Negro race now in America is derived from an admixture of people of various African tribes, probably differing considerably among themselves, but all, it may be assumed, in a more or less savage and little civilised condition. They have all passed two or three generations in slavery to white men, during which period all traces of their various origin have been lost, as well as their original languages and habits. And now, though variety of breed, affecting their capacity, may still to some degree be present, if we could trace it, I believe that it is impossible to do so, and that we must deal with them as a single, English-speaking people. They are also now all Christians; and though some African traditions may linger among them, they have for the most part adopted the dress and manners of their white masters, and have been greatly civilised. In this latter respect there is, however, a considerable distinction. One portion of the Negroes has lived in parts of the country where the white population was numerous—equal to or more numerous than the blacks—and thus, working among and in very intimate contact with white people, has very thoroughly learned their ways, habits, and ideas. But there is a broad belt round the outer portion of the Southern States where the climate is very injurious to the white man, and almost impossible to the ordinary white labourer. In this tract, containing much of the most productive country, the whole labouring population was and is Negro, the few white men being, in slave times, only the masters and drivers, and in no degree the comrades of the blacks. In these tracts we have a thick population not so completely converted. Their language is still to some degree a sort of pigeon or Negro English, and they are still to some extent a peculiar people—perhaps less good workers than those more thoroughly educated by contact with whites, but probably as a rule more simple and docile. It should be noticed, however, that considerable migrations have taken place in the troubles consequent on the war, and that there has been some intermixture of the two classes.

At the time of emancipation the Negroes were destitute of education to an excessive degree. Not only were means of education wanting to them, but after some local troubles which alarmed the masters most of the Southern States passed laws making it highly penal to educate a Negro. These laws endured to the last, and under them the generation upon whom emancipation came grew up entirely without instruction.The only educated persons of the race were the few free blacks who had obtained instruction in the North, and a very few favourite domestic slaves, whom their mistresses had to some degree educated, the penal laws notwithstanding. Since emancipation a good deal has been done to educate the Negro. Many schools in which a superior education is afforded have been maintained by benevolent Northerners, and the State Governments have set up, and continue to maintain, several colleges in which the more ambitious and aspiring young blacks are educated. For the education of the masses a public school system has been started in all the States, of which the blacks have a fair share. Owing, however, to financial difficulties these schools are extremely imperfect, being open but a small portion of each year—in some States as little as two months, and in none, I believe, more than about four months on an average. However, this is better than nothing. The Negroes show a laudable zeal for education, and upon the whole I think that as much has been done as could be expected under the circumstances.

During the last dozen years the Negroes have had a very large share of political education. Considering the troubles and the ups and downs that they have gone through, it is, I think, wonderful how beneficial this education has been to them, and how much these people, so lately in the most debased condition of slavery, have acquired independent ideas, and, far from lapsing into anarchy, have become citizens with ideas of law and property and order. The white serfs of European countries took hundreds of years to rise to the level which these Negroes have attained in a dozen. Such has been the thoroughness of the measures adopted in America.

Another education has, I think, greatly affected the character and self-reliance of the Negroes. I mean what I may call their religious education. Like most primitive races (the aborigines of India, for instance) they are inclined to take Christianity in a more literal sense than their more civilised fellow-Christians, who have managed to explain most of it away to their own satisfaction. And these Negroes are by temperament extremely religious people of an emotional type. They like to go direct to God himself, and are quite unwilling to submit to priests claiming to stand between them and God. Hence it is that the Catholic hierarchy has had no success with them, and probably never will have. Every man and woman likes to be himself or herself an active member of the Church. And though their preachers are in a great degree their leaders, these preachers are chosen by the people from the people, under a system for the most part congregational, and are rather preachers because they are leaders than leaders because they are preachers. In this matter of religion the Negroes have utterly emancipated themselves from all white guidance—they have their own churches and their own preachers, all coloured men—and the share they take in the self-government of their churches really is a very important education. The preachers to our eyes may seem peculiar. American orators somewhat exaggerate and emphasize our style, and the black preachers somewhat exaggerate the American style; but on the whole I felt considerably edified by them. They come to the point in a way that is refreshing after some sermons that one has heard. I did not witness any of the more active emotions in which I understand congregations sometimes indulge; but the practice of emitting in a hearty way a sort of responses here and there during the sermon seemed to me earnest and not unbecoming. I witnessed a convention of Baptist ministers (the blacks generally are Baptists or Methodists), in a rural church, and it was a pleasant sight. The ministers by no means had it all their own way. The whole country-side seemed to have come in to assist, both men and women—and they seemed to be making a time of it—camped about for the day.

The prominent position taken by the Negro women is a feature in which they are distinguished from some Oriental races. No doubt this has some advantages, but also I shall have to note some attendant disadvantages —social, industrial, and political. In matters matrimonial the women are somewhat too independent and light hearted; and the men also being on this subject given to a rather loose philosophy, the marital tie is not so binding and indissoluble as it might be. Those who take an unfavourable view of the Negro character are in the habit of speaking of these traits of their character in severe language, and dwelling much on their immorality and want of family affection. I think, however, that it is scarcely fair to judge them by too high a standard. The truth is that the Aryan family has hardly yet established itself among the Negroes, and it is not surprising that this should be so. In Africa we know that nothing of the kind exists; there, no doubt, the progenitors of the American blacks lived under the loose polygamistic system still prevailing there. Under slavery the family could not be introduced—it was impossible that there could be much permanency of marital arrangements when the parties were constantly liable to be, and very frequently were, sold away like cattle; and the relation between parent and child was especially weakened, or rather not created. The parents were not really responsible for the children; on the contrary, the women were sent to work, and the children were carefully tended by persons appointed by the masters for the purpose, like calves or lambs or any other valuable stock. Parents had little affection for children thus reared, and children owed no respect and obedience to parents. The family as we know it is, in fact, a novelty to the Negro since emancipation, and such institutions are not perfected in a day. Still the evil is a very grave one, especially in regard to the relations between parents and children. I have heard many authentic stories of children who have deserted or neglected their parents in a shocking manner, and the more than American liberty of the children threatens to render the next generation less tractable and useful than their fathers bred in slavery. We can only hope that time and religious influences will more completely establish the family system. Though the exceptions are many, there seems already to be much that is good and kind in the relations of the blacks to one another. If in some respects, other than marital, the women are rather troublesome, it seems that in this as in other things they have rather exaggerated American ways than set up ways of their own. Seeing the liberty, equality, and privileges enjoyed by the free white women, the Negro women insist that their position among their own race shall not be inferior.

Reverting now to the capacities of the Negro as we find him in America under the circumstances which I have described, the general opinion of those engaged in the education of the race is, that while the younger children are as quick and bright as white children, they do on the average fall off in some degree as they get older. Yet this opinion is not given without some consideration and qualification; the intellectual gulf between the two races does not seem to be very wide and evident. I am told on all hands that some pure Negroes show an educational capacity quite equal to that of good whites. Nothing is more difficult than to estimate accurately qualities of this kind, especially when, as in this case, the two classes are not taught together, but separately; and there has not yet been time to see much of the results of educating the blacks on a large scale; but I think that in general terms the direction in which all experience points is that which I have stated, viz., that on the whole they are behind, but not very far behind.

When we look to practical success in life appearances seem at first sight less favourable to the blacks. I constantly asked, "Have any individuals among them come to the front and achieved success in industrial pursuits, in commerce, or in the professions?" and I could not learn that they have. "There were," I said, "before the war a number of free blacks, many of them educated; have none of them distinguished themselves in practical life? And since emancipation the Negroes have for years had the upper hand in some of the Southern States; have none of them come to the front among their own race by the process of natural selection which has raised men to greatness in barbarous and Oriental countries?" Well, as I have already mentioned, they have shown some capacity as preachers, and they seem to have some talent for oratory (though I believe that Frederick Douglass and one or two other well-known men are mulattos, not real Negroes). As politicians some of them have done fairly well, and are now good and popular representatives of their race; but I don't think any of them have made a great mark. The politics of the Southern States, while Negro majorities prevailed, seem to have been in reality entirely under the guidance of the white "Carpet-baggers."

For the rest I have not been able to hear of a successful Negro merchant —the shopkeeping business in the most Negro districts is almost entirely in the hands of whites. I have scarcely found a Negro who has risen in the mercantile world higher than an apple-stall in a market. Certain professions they almost monopolise throughout the Union—waiters and barbers, and in some parts ship-caulkers; but I found very few Negro lawyers, and no doctors. All over the world it is curious to notice how ready people are to entrust the care of their souls to very unsafe home-rulers, and how much less trustful they are of their bodies.

When I have put these failures to the friends of the Negroes they reply that allowance must be made for very great disadvantages—even in the North, they say, the free Negroes were subjected to a social ostracism which made their success in commerce and the professions almost impossible. And as regards the South, they say, "Since emancipation how short a time has elapsed!—people enslaved and denied education cannot rise in a day." In all this there is much truth. Still I cannot help thinking that if the race had been a very pushing and capable one, the men educated in the North would ere this have made more way in the South. "Do you think," I have said, "that if they had been Chinamen they would not, in spite of all these disadvantages, have found their way to the front in some directions?" I think it is admitted that to some extent this is so. The Negroes are certainly not a race remarkable for energy and force under difficulties. The only question is whether they are very deficient in these qualities. As respects mercantile qualities, we may remember that there are many excellent races who show no aptitude that way and permit alien races to usurp the mercantile functions. In the Southern States the white Americans themselves are very much ousted from the business of small storekeepers by the Germans, who are to the manner born.

What is more disappointing is the failure of the Negroes, so far, as superior artisans and in all that requires accuracy and care. As it is expressed, they are not *responsible*—they cannot be depended on. In slavery times some of them were pretty good artisans, and many of them, in the South, are now fairly good carpenters, bricklayers, and blacksmiths. But they seem hardly to have progressed in this respect since emancipation. A man who will do his carpentry so far well enough will not fit the pieces accurately; and in factories which employ black labour they do not rise to higher posts. In the North the trades unions are so strong, and the jealousy of the Negroes on the part of foreigners, Irish and others, is so great, that they would not have a fair chance; but in the South they labour under no such disadvantage, and employers rather prefer Negro labour; yet in practice they don't seem to be able to trust the blacks beyond a certain point. In mechanical shops the blacks do the manual labour, but are hardly trusted to work engines. "Perhaps a Negro might learn to work the engine," an employer said to me, 'but I never could be sure that he would not go to sleep on the top of it." In tobacco factories the labour is almost exclusively Negro, and many of them are very well paid for labour requiring considerable skill; but I noticed that for certain work, the weighing and making up the packages and such-like, white men were always employed. I was in all these cases assured that no black man could be trusted to be accurate. Yet they make very fair cotton-farmers, and much of their handiwork in various branches of industry is quite good.

On the whole, I think it must be considered that at present, whether from natural defects or from want of cultivation, they are to a certain extent inferior to white men in the qualities which lead to the higher grades of employment. On the other hand, they have a very remarkable good nature and good temper, much docility, and great physical power and endurance—qualities that admirably fit them for labourers. Considering from how low and oppressed a condition they have been lately raised, and how infinitely higher their position now is, it is hardly ground for disappointment that they do not immediately rise in large numbers to the higher grades of society. They have now opportunities of education which will enable them to rise, if they are fitted or when they are fitted for it.

12: BLACK DILEMMAS IN THE 1890s

*Rights which the agricultural labourers of England
did not obtain till 1885 were in 1867 thrust upon
these children of nature, whose highest form of
pleasure had hitherto been to caper to the strains
of a banjo.*

James Bryce (1838-1922), public official and Oxford University law
professor, made four visits to the United States before service as English
ambassador to this country, 1907-13. In 1883, after a third trip, the
Irishman began work on his classic study *The American Commonwealth*
(1888), which was later revised to include research compiled during subsequent visits. Bryce attempted a thorough investigation of the American
system. He toured many regions of the country, including the South and
West in 1881. Bryce analyzed almost every facet of black institutional life,
and saw limited progress for a race he deemed "uncivilized" and primitive.
The following selection is from the 1895 revised edition, based on Bryce's
1890 trip.

The total coloured population of the United States was in 1890
7,470,040, a number greater than that of the English people in the reign
of Queen Anne, and one which might anywhere but in North America be
deemed to form a considerable nation. Of this total, seven millions (in
round numbers) were in the old Slave States, and it is of these only that
the present chapter will speak.

Of the economic and industrial state of the whole seven millions it is
hard to speak in general terms, so different are the conditions which different

Lord James Bryce, *The American Commonwealth* (London, Macmillan and Co.,
1895), 3rd edition, vol. 2, pp. 491-509.

parts of the country present. In one point only are those conditions uniform. Everywhere, alike in the Border States and the farthest South, in the cities, both great and small, and in the rural districts, the coloured population constitute the poorest and socially lowest stratum, corresponding in this respect to the new immigrants in the Northern States, although, as we shall presently observe, they are far more sharply and permanently divided than are those immigrants from the classes above them. They furnish nine-tenths of the unskilled labour, and a still larger proportion of the domestic and hotel labour. Some, though a comparatively small number, have found their way into the skilled handicrafts, such as joinery and metal work; and many are now employed in the mines and iron foundries of South-eastern Tennessee and Northern Alabama, where they receive wages sometimes equal to those paid to the white workmen, and are even occasionally admitted to the same trade-unions.[1] In textile factories they are deemed decidedly inferior to the whites; the whirr of the machinery is said to daze them or to send them to sleep. On the other hand, they handle tobacco better than the whites, and practically monopolize this large industry. In all the cities a great part of the small retail trade is in their hands, as are also such occupations as those of barber, shoe-black, street vendor of drinks or fruit, together with the humbler kinds of railway service. In the rural districts the immense majority are either hired labourers or tenants of small farms, the latter class becoming more numerous the further south one goes into the hot and malarious regions, where the white man is less disposed to work on his own land. Of these tenants many—and some are both active and thrifty—cultivate upon a system of crop-sharing, like that of the *métayers* in France. Not a few have bought plots of land, and work it for themselves. Of those who farm either their own land, or that for which they pay rent, an increasing number are raising crops for the market, and steadily improving their condition. Others, however, are content with getting from the soil enough food to keep their families; and this is more especially the case in the lower lands along the coast, where the population is almost wholly black, and little affected by the influences either of commerce or of the white race. In these hot lowlands the Negro lives much as he lived on the plantations in the old days, except that he works less, because a moderate amount of labour produces enough for his bare subsistence. No railway comes near him. He sees no newspaper: he is scarcely at all in contact with any one above his own condition. Thus there are places, the cities especially, where the Negro is improving industrially, because he has to work hard and comes into constant relation with the whites; and other places, where he need work very little, and where, being left to his own resources, he is in danger of relapsing into barbarism. These differences in his material progress in different parts of the country must be constantly borne in mind when one attempts to form a picture of his present intellectual and moral state.

The phenomena he presents in this latter aspect are absolutely new in the annals of the world. History is a record of the progress towards civilization of races originally barbarous. But that progress has in all previous cases been slow and gradual. In the case of the chief Asiatic and European races, the earlier stages are lost in the mists of antiquity. Even the middle and later stages, as we gather them from the writings of the historians of antiquity and from the records of the Dark and Middle Ages, show an advance in which there is nothing sudden or abrupt, but rather a process of what may be called tentative development, the growth and enlargement of the human mind resulting in and being accompanied by a gradual improvement of political institutions and of the arts and sciences. In this process there are no leaps and bounds; and it is the work, not of any one race alone, but of the mingled rivalry and co-operation of several. Utterly dissimilar is the case of the African Negro, caught up in and whirled along with the swift movement of the American democracy. In it we have a singular juxtaposition of the most primitive and the most recent, the most rudimentary and the most highly developed, types of culture. Not greater is the interval which separates the chipped flints of the Stone Age from the Maxim gun of to-day. A body of savages is violently carried across the ocean and set to work as slaves on the plantations of masters who are three or four thousand years in advance of them in mental capacity and moral force. They are treated like horses or oxen, are kept at labour by the lash, are debarred from even the elements of education, have no more status before the law, no more share in the thought of the culture of their owner than the sheep which he shears. The children and grandchildren of those whom the slave-ship brought to the plantation remain like their parents, save indeed that they have learnt a new and highly developed tongue and have caught up so much of a new religion as comes to them through preachers of their own blood. Those who have housework to do, or who live in the few and small towns, pick up some knowledge of white ways, and imitate them to the best of their power. But the great mass remain in their notions and their habits much what their ancestors were in the forests of the Niger or the Congo. Suddenly, even more suddenly than they were torn from Africa, they find themselves, not only freed, but made full citizens and active members of the most popular government the world has seen, treated as fit to bear an equal part in ruling, not themselves only, but also their recent masters. Rights which the agricultural labourers of England did not obtain till 1885 were in 1867 thrust upon these children of nature, whose highest form of pleasure had hitherto been to caper to the strains of a banjo.

This tremendous change arrested one set of influences that were telling on the Negro, and put another set in motion. The relation of master and servant came to an end, and with it the discipline of compulsory labour and a great part of such intercourse as there had been between the white and the black races. Very soon the whites began to draw away from the Negro, who became less a friend in fact the more he was an equal in theory. Presently the mixture of blood stopped, a mixture which had been doing something for the blacks in leavening their mass,—only slightly on the plantations, but to some extent in the towns and among the domestic servants,—with persons of superior energy and talent. On the other hand, there were immediately turned on the freedman a volume of new forces which had scarcely affected him as a slave. He had now to care for himself, in sickness and in health. He might go where he would, and work as much or as little as he pleased. He had a vote to give or to sell. Education became accessible; and facilities for obtaining it were promptly accorded to him, first by his Northern liberators, but soon by his old masters also. As he learned to read and to vote, a crowd of modern American ideas, political, social, religious, and economic, poured in upon him through the newspapers. No such attempt has ever been made before to do for a race at one stroke what in other times and countries nature has spent centuries in doing. Other races have desired freedom and a share in political power. They have had to strive, and their efforts have braced and disciplined them. But these things were thrust upon the Negro, who found himself embarrassed by boons he had not thought of demanding.

To understand how American ideas work in an African brain, and how American institutions are affecting African habits, one must consider what are the character and gifts of the Negro himself.

He is by nature affectionate, docile, pliable, submissive, and in these respects most unlike the Red Indian, whose conspicuous traits are pride and a certain dogged inflexibility. He is seldom cruel or vindictive—which the Indian often is—nor is he prone to violence, except when spurred by lust. His intelligence is rather quick than solid; and though not wanting in a sort of shrewdness, he shows the childishness as well as the lack of self-control which belongs to the primitive peoples. A nature highly impressionable, emotional, and unstable is in him appropriately accompanied by a love of music, while for art he has—unlike the Red Indian—no taste or turn whatever. Such talent as he has runs to words; he learns languages easily and writes and speaks fluently, but shows no capacity for abstract thinking, for scientific inquiry, or for any kind of invention. It is, however, not so conspicuously on the intellectual side that his weakness lies, as in the sphere of will and action. Having neither foresight nor "roundsight," he is heedless and unthrifty, easily elated and depressed, with little tenacity of purpose, and but a feeble wish to better his condition. Sloth, like that into which the Negroes of the Antilles have sunk, cannot be generally charged upon the American coloured man, partly perhaps because the climate is less enervating and nature less bountiful. Although not so steady a workman as is the white, he is less troublesome to his employers, because less disposed to strike. It is by his toil that a large part of the cotton, rice, and sugar crop of the South is now raised.

Among the modes or avenues in and by which the influences of white America are moulding the Negro, [three] deserve to be specially noted, those of the schools, . . . of literature, and of industry. . . .

Looking merely at the figures, elementary education would seem to have made extraordinary progress. In the former Slave States there are now 52 per cent of the coloured population of school age enrolled on the books of some school, the percentage of white pupils to the white population of school age in the same States being 67, and the percentage of enrolments to population over the whole United States 69.[2] In these States the coloured people are 30.98 per cent of the total population, and the coloured pupils 27.37 per cent of the total school enrolments. A smaller percentage of them than of white children is, therefore, on the books of the schools; but when it is remembered that thirty-five years ago only an infinitesimally small percentage were at school at all, and that in many States it was a penal offence to teach a Negro to read, the progress made is remarkable. Between 1877 and 1889, while the white pupils in the common schools of the South increased 70 per cent, the coloured pupils increased 113 per cent. It must not, however, be concluded from these figures that nearly the whole of the coloured population are growing up possessed even of the rudiments of education. The ratio of attendance to school enrolment is, indeed, almost as good for the Negroes as for the whites (62.14 against 62.48), the Negroes, both parents and children, having a desire for instruction. But the school-terms are so short in most of the Southern States—the average number of days' schooling in the year for each pupil being only 100 for the South-eastern States, and 95 for the South-western against 168 in the North-eastern—that a large number of whites and a still larger number of coloured children receive too little teaching to enable them to read and write with ease. Thus out of 4,759,040 Negroes in the old Slave States over ten years of age, 2,887,826, or nearly 61 per cent, are returned as illiterates.[3] That the amount of higher education—seminary, collegiate, or university education—obtained by the Negroes is not only absolutely small, but incomparably smaller than that obtained by the whites, is no more than might be expected from the fact that they constitute the poorest part of the population. The total number of institutions of this description was in 1891 as follows:[4]

Normal schools	52,	with	10,042 pupils.
Secondary schools	47,	with	11,837 pupils.
Universities and colleges[5]	25,	with	8,396 pupils.
Schools of theology	25,	with	755 pupils.
Schools of law	5,	with	121 pupils.
Schools of medicine, dentistry, pharmacy	5,	with	306 pupils.
Schools for the deaf and dumb and the blind	16,	with	536 pupils.

These universities are, of course, on a comparatively humble scale, and most of them might rather be called secondary schools. To these figures I may add that the grants made by the State governments to common schools—in the South it is usually from the State treasury and not from local taxation that school funds are derived—are generally distributed equally to white and to coloured schools: a circumstance which appears the more creditable to the good feeling and wisdom of the ruling whites when it is remembered that since they hold nearly all the property, they pay by far the larger part of the taxes, State and local. These funds, how-ever, nearly all go to elementary education, and the institutions which provide higher education for the Negro are quite unequal to the demands made upon them. Swarms of applicants for admission have to be turned away from the already over-crowded existing upper and normal schools and colleges; and thus the supply of qualified teachers for the coloured schools is greatly below the needs of the case. The total number is at present only 24,150, with 1,324,937 pupils to deal with. In the white schools, with 3,539,670 pupils, there are 79,062 teachers, a proportion (about 1 teacher to 44 pupils) obviously much too low, and too low even if we allow for the difference between enrolment and attendance. But the proportion in the coloured schools is lower still (1 to 53), and the teachers themselves are less instructed. The need for secondary and normal schools is, therefore, still urgent, though much has been and is being done by Northern benevo-lence for this admirable purpose. There is something pathetic in the eager-ness of the Negroes, parents, young people, and children, to obtain instruc-tion. They seem to think that the want of it is what keeps them below the whites, just as in the riots which broke out in South Carolina during Sher-man's invasion, the Negro mob burnt a library at Columbia because, as they said, it was from the books that "the white folks got their sense." And they have a notion (which, to be sure, is not confined to them) that it is the want of book-learning which condemns the vast bulk of their race to live by manual labor, and that, therefore, by acquiring such learning they may themselves rise in the industrial scale.

From what has been said of the state of education, it will have been gathered that the influence of books is confined to extremely few, and that even of newspapers to a small fraction of the coloured people. Nevertheless, the significance of whatever forms the mind of that small fraction must not be underestimated. The few thousands who read books or magazines, the few tens of thousands who see a daily paper, acquire the ideas and beliefs and aspirations of the normal white citizen, subject of course to the inherent differences in race character already referred to. They are in a sense more American than the recent immigrants from Central Europe and from Italy, who are now a substantial element in the population of the Middle and Western States. Within this small section of the coloured people are the natural leaders of the millions who have not yet attained to what may be called the democratic American consciousness. And the number of those upon whom books and newspapers play, in whom democratic ideas stimulate discontent with the present inferiority of their people, is steadily, and in some districts, rapidly increasing. The efforts of those who are best fitted to lead have been hitherto checked by the jealousy which the mass is apt to feel for those who rise to prominence; but this tendency may decline, and there will be no reason for surprise if men of eloquence and ambition are one day found to give voice to the sentiments of their brethren as Frederick Douglass did.[6]

The influence of industry is another name for the influence of self-help. As a slave the Negro was no doubt taught to give steady, though unintelligent, labour; and this was probably a step forward from his condition in Africa. But labour all of it performed under supervision, and none of it followed by any advantage to the labourer except relief from the lash, labour whose aim was to accomplish not the best possible but the least that would suffice, did nothing to raise the character or to train the intelligence. Every day's work that the Negro has done since he became a freeman has helped him. Most of the work is rough work, whether on the land or in the cities, and is done for low wages. But the number of those who, either as owners or as tenant farmers, raise their own crops for the market, and of those who are finding their way into skilled employments, is an always increasing number. I have seen it stated that in 1892 the Southern Negroes paid taxes on property valued at more than $14,000,000, practically all of which has been acquired since 1865. To raise crops for the market is an education in thrift, foresight, and business aptitude, as well as in agriculture; to follow a skilled industry is to train the intelligence as well as the hand, and the will as well as the intelligence. There is, unfortunately, very little provision for the instruction of the young Negroes in any handicraft, and the need of means for imparting it is even more urgent than is that of secondary schools. It is satisfactory to know that the necessity is beginning to be recognized, and some effort made to provide industrial training. Dr. W. T. Harris observes with perfect truth:

With better industrial habits there comes a better style of living. Though most of the Negroes still live in rude cabins, no better than the huts which served them as slaves, they who own or rent land have begun to erect decent houses, and furnish them with taste, while in the suburbs of a city the Negro tradesman has sometimes as neat a villa as the white of like occupation, though generally obliged to inhabit the coloured quarter.

Against the industrial progress of the Negro there must be set two depressing phenomena. One is the increase of insanity, very marked during the last few decades, and probably attributable to the increased facilities which freedom has given for obtaining liquor, and to the stress which independence and education have imposed on the undeveloped brain of a backward race. The other, not unconnected with the former, is the large amount of crime. Most of it is petty crime, chiefly thefts of hogs and poultry, but there are also a good many crimes against women. Seventy per cent of the convicts in Southern jails are Negroes,[7] and though one must allow for the fact that they are the poorest part of the population and that the law is probably more strictly enforced against them than against the whites, this is a proportion double that of their numbers.[8] Even in the District of Columbia more than half the arrests are among the coloured people, though they are only one third of the inhabitants.

NOTES

1. I find it stated (1893) that in West Tennessee the average pay per day of the skilled white labourer is $2.50, of the coloured $1.60; and conceive that this may fairly represent the proportion in most trades, though perhaps less in mining than in some others. A large employer of labour in Virginia assured me in 1890 that he paid some of his Negroes (iron-workers) as much as $4.50 per day. He added that they worked along with the whites, and drank less.
2. *Report of the Commissioner of Education for 1890-91*, vol. 2.
3. Abstract of the census of 1890, Table 14.
   The proportion of illiterates is highest in South Caroline (64.1 per cent), Georgia (67.3), Alabama (69.1), and Louisiana (72.1); lowest in the District of Columbia (35), and Oklahoma (39.2). The Territory of Oklahoma was not a Slave State, but its Negro population (only 2,290 over ten years of age) is very small, and consists of Negroes who have recently arrived from the older South.
4. *Report of the Commissioner of Education for 1890-91*, p. 1962.
5. Including preparatory and primary departments of universities.
6. I remember to have listened to a striking speech by a Negro in Richmond in which he appealed to the historic glories of the State of Virginia, and sought to rouse the audience by reminding them that they too were Virginians.

7. The South is still far behind the North in matters of prison management. Convicts, and sometimes white as well as coloured convicts, are in many States hired out to private employers or companies for rough work, and very harshly treated.

8. It must however be observed that in the rest of the Union (North East, North Central, and West), the proportion of prisoners in the jails is much higher among the foreign born than in the population at large, doubtless because they are the poorest class. The foreign born are 20 per cent of the population and constitute 37 per cent of the prisoners. The foreign born and children of foreign parents, taken together, constitute 49 per cent of the prisoners.

JAN and CORA GORDON

13: BLACK MUSIC AND CHURCH LIFE
IN NORTH CAROLINA

*The collection came while we were all yet under the
spell. The big preacher, eyeing the congregation, almost demanded their money and their faith.*

The English artists Jan and Cora Gordon toured the east coast in 1927,
spending some time in the southern states, experiencing various aspects of
black cultural life. While in North Carolina, they attended a church meeting
and were impressed with the singing and the minister's spiritual impact on
his congregation.

The church was in the dark unlighted street typical of the Negro quarter.
However, there it was at last, its windows glowing gently in prismatic
colours, a shadowy congregation climbing up its steps with the delibera-
tion of habitual church goers and spilling voluble gossip before a churchly
silence should seal their lips.

A lean and ascetic looking coloured minister met us at the church door
and introduced us with ceremony to the fat preacher for the evening, and
for the first time we learned the guise in which we were welcomed.

"I have to present to you the Reverend Jeremiah Sampson," said the
minister. "This is Professor Gordon of scholastic interests attached to the
Educational Department—and his good lady."

You have to hear the Negro minister's intonation to get the full value
of my new dignity—"scho-lastic . . . Ed-dew-cayshe-o-nal . . . Dee-part-ment,"
but in the Reverend Saunders' mouth it had an even richer quality. He was

Jan and Cora Gordon, *On Wandering Wheels* (London, Bodley Head, 1929), pp. 303–
10, 313–14. Reprinted by permission of the publisher.

a big man, and the great Negro voice boomed from him, inspiring in its very sonority.

The church was finer than we had expected. It was amphitheatral and the circular rows of ascending pews faced a raised dais on which was a carved lectern of the design popularly supposed to be pleasing to the Trinity. A curved balustrade protected the dais from the congregation, and between platform and rails stood a table with a dish. A raised stall for the choir stood to the left of the dais. The two clergymen sat in stately chairs on the dais, while five young men with coloured bands on their arms arranged themselves in the choir stalls. The congregation, few in number and mostly middle aged and rather hopeless women in clothes as black as their faces, spotted themselves in the ample pew space. The ascetic old minister surveyed their small numbers with a smile of gentle understanding.

"We had hoped tonight to have with us some of the choirs competing in song," he said, "but we had overlooked that tonight is the last night of the coloured people's fair. As this is their one great celebration of the year we behove us brethren not to stigmatize them for wishing to take advantage of the opportunity. Which also accounts for the comparative paucity of the congregation. But we must be very, very grateful that the Quartet has thoughtfully not deserted us and in consideration of the Quartet's kindness we have engaged not to prolong the service that they may get back to their very natural and innocent enjoyment before it closes. Let us now offer a prayer, brethren."

The service proceeded with simplicity until the sermon. Then the big preacher arose and flung open the Bible with a gesture.

"Brothers and sisters—" he gave a little extra bow in our direction as though conscious that though he must include us yet he understood that we might hold ourselves a shade higher in the sight of God—"I am going to prove to you tonight infallibly, against the arguments of the sceptics, the undoubted Divinity of Jesus Christ."

He began with restraint. We, thinking of the occupants of the pews behind, wondered what they were making of the sermon. We cannot suppose that one member of that flock had any suspicion that the Divinity of Christ had been impugned, or knew what sceptics were. Bringing faith to that congregation was indeed bringing coals to Newcastle. The Preacher's words flowed at first with unexpected precision; he had studied evidently both grammar and rhetoric. But, as he went deeper and deeper into his subject his voice increased in volume and every sentence leapt from his mouth in a veritable roar; his gestures increased in enthusiasm until he was stamping about the platform, shaking his great fists at the unbeliever, and the perspiration was pouring down his face. He hit the pulpit so that, had it not been made of solid ecclesiastical stuff, it would have split under his blows. He shouted, leapt, banged, and gesticulated until disbelief was impossible. And then, having slain every sceptical argument which he could invent—though none of the true ones—as if with the blows of a huge club, he gave one last exulting howl of triumph, a last bison's bellow of defiance at any unbeliever yet lurking in the darkness, and subsided onto his chair, where he pulled out a big handkerchief and mopped his face. The thin minister then rose and, in a voice very faint after that tornado of elocution, challenged any unbeliever to rise and refute the reverend's magnificent array of truths. It was as if the valiant little tailor had challenged the nine flies to rise up and sip his jam once more. They were swotted.

The collection came while we were all yet under the spell. The big preacher, eyeing the congregation, almost demanded their money *and* their faith. Now we understood the object of the smaller table between the balustrade and the dais. A little old well dressed Negro stepped forward to it and laid a fifty cent piece in the dish, and one or two others in turn contributed. I also walked out and added our offering. The preacher, who was keeping a sharp eye on the plate, made a trumpet of his hands and through them rasped in a hoarse aside to the people:

"Brethren, the professor's given a dollar."

Under the power of the preacher's eye one by one the members laid down their mites. If anyone thought of avoiding his duty the Reverend fixed him or her with a glower until, creeping forward, that member paid up. When the last nickel had been deposited, the preacher picked up the plate and, stirring it with his fingers, counted the contents. He put it back on the table.

"There's four dollars and twenty cents," he announced; "now I'm not saying that that isn't a fine collection for this meeting, thanks to the generosity of our white friend, Professor Gordon of scholastic interests attached to the Educational Department, who we have here with us tonight accompanied by his good lady; but, brethren, what I wants is to see that raised to five dollars. We wants eighty cents more, brethren. Eighty cents more to make a round sum for the glory of God. . . ."

He beat out the changes on eighty cents and five dollars until the little old man brought out another nickel.

"Thank you, brother. Seventy-five cents now . . . only seventy-five. . . . Thank you, sister. . . . Only seventy. . . . Thank you, lady . . . thank you (to Jo) another twenty-five, this is generosity . . . only forty-five . . . only forty-five. . . ."

We refrained from filling up the five dollars because we did not wish to bring this scene to an abrupt conclusion. Then the quartet, who as a matter of fact were five, after some whispering, came up one by one and each in turn shyly contributed. This was evidently an unusual proceeding; the preacher was profuse in his gratitude. Also, he announced that they had generously forgone the percentage of the collection which was their customary fee.

Nevertheless fifteen cents remained to be found, and for a time all the preacher's eloquence was powerless to extract it from the members. After ten minutes we were still the fifteen cents short.

Suddenly the preacher, with a huge bellow, stabbed his long finger at the little old Negro.

"Thar's a brudder feelin' in his pocket," he shouted. "Brudder, a man what feels in his pocket is lost. Brudder, I calls on you to make up that fifteen cents. That fifteen cents is yours. . . ."

The poor old man, feeling very publicly exposed, continued to hunt through his pockets, but not one nickel of change could he find. At last a look of resolution dawned on his polished face. He stepped up to the table, pulled open his trousers pocket to its widest extent, poured the whole collection into it, shook the weight comfortably down and, with a gesture of finality, slapped a five dollar note onto the table. The collection was closed.

Indeed a collection of one pound English from that congregation was a feat remarkable enough; at least three times as much as could be collected from a similar set of people in similar positions in England. Moreover Negroes are not paid the large wages of the white American working man.

In spite of the interest of the sermon and of the collection we had been feeling cheated by the absence of the "shape note" singers; but now the quartet (or more correctly, quintet) paid us for our journey, in full measure. The five men gathered in a close circle, their faces together as though about to whisper confidences. Then the leader threw back his head and announced the first line melodiously. Evidently the choice had been inspired by the sermon which had insisted strongly on the medical powers of Christ.

> Oh, He a-raisin' up Lazarus
>   Yes, raisin' him up,
> Raisin' him up from de dead,
>   Yes, dat's what He done.
> And all de folks was watching roun',
> Jedus bring up Lazarus f'um under de groun'
> An' say him, "Go prophesy;"
> An' say him, "Go prophesy."
>
> De sick He goan to heal,
>   Yes, He heal 'em;
> De blin' He make to see,
>   Yes, dat's a fac'.

He done able de cripple to walk
An' make de dumb man to talk.
An' say to him, "Go prophesy;"
An' say to him, "Go prophesy."

We had heard the Fisk singers in Paris, and other trained spiritual choirs on the gramophone records, but this choir had something which we had expected to find in Negro singing and had hitherto not found. . . . Well, here it was at last. Even "the shouters" of Charlotte had not this peculiar and essential Negro quality. The four members of the quartet sang in the "Spiritual" harmonies to which published versions have accustomed us, but the fifth, with a strong high tenor voice, threw across the harmonies of the four blended voices a wild counterpart, an improvisation which gave the singing a new quality, a dramatic intensity, sweeping it away from that humble little church in the slum of a Carolinian town and carrying it far into the African wilderness. The medicine man may have sung with that voice. What gave an additional peculiarity to the spiritual was that at times, now and again, the singers rose and fell, slurring in harmony, so that they seemed to be singing in quarter tone chords at times. Yes, this was a singing which was worth the trouble of coming a distance to hear.

They sang some four songs, all in the same inspiring and wild way. Then suddenly to my perturbation and amazement the preacher announced:

"Brethren, we have tonight with us, with great pleasure, our white friends, Professor Gordon of scholastic interests attached to the Educational Department and his good lady. Now, dear brethren, we hope that the Professor will be so kind and give the brethren a few comfortin' words."

This announcement took me fully aback. I had not come prepared to make a speech; promiscuous eloquence is far from my habit or practise. But I suddenly felt that I must not disappoint the church; for the honour, at least, of the Educational Department I was bound to say something. But what to say? The singing still rang in my ears and I suddenly thought of the Fisk singers, how they had betrayed their racial talent by Westernising their songs. So ascending the dais I talked on that theme. I am convinced it was as far above my audience's head as the preacher's sermon; but of course the less they understood of it the more profound they would believe it to be. Negroes are not different from other people. Those scrub-women and wives tired with household duties could not understand what propaganda for the Negro race implied; nor what signified preserving the qualities of a racial talent. We had been reading an article which told how, under the lash of white man's humour, the Negro had become self-conscious; he avoided chickens, watermelons, spirituals, pigs' feet, coloured clothes, pork chops, razors and so on. He is afraid to be consciously a Negro; not seeing that his only chance of salvation socially is to insist that he is himself, to build himself deliberately yet subtly into one of the racial elements of the new America. Yes, well above their heads, I preached my first sermon to myself and babbled into shape thoughts which had been hitherto only vague ideas in my mind.

The service was over. We had to give each member of the church the honour of a handshake. Then we had also a short talk with the choir leader. He seemed quite aware of the peculiar quality of his music, assured us that he intended to preserve it and had no wish to Westernise it. . . . We said good night to the contrasted ministers, found the old "Hearse" and trundled back through the darkness to our suite in the coloured girls' college.

. . . .

The position of the Negro was perhaps even more clearly emphasized in the next town where we halted, always looking for the shape note singing. Here we called on the head of a smaller school which stood under the shadow of a cotton mill. There had been trouble in the town because, after a Ku Klux demonstration, the white children were amusing themselves by pushing the coloured ones off the pavements into the gutter. Some of the more spirited Negro boys were planning reprisals.

"We had to stop them at once," said the Principal. "You see, anything might start a riot. The workers in that cotton mill are poor whites, come down from the mountains, and we live in constant terror of them. For a trifle that whole factory might get excited and come pouring into here to destroy the whole place."

We could understand their terror. You must have been in the South to understand the pure, sinister quality of the word "lynch." In the streets those close eyed, thin lipped loafers stare with something inhuman in their gaze. They are like no people anywhere else; they have the faces of jaguars. Interbreeding, poverty, fever, and laziness are obstacles enough for any race to contend against; add to this the competition of the Negro race, which is bound to undersell the white merely because no white man will pay it a white man's wages. There is the cause of the poverty and idleness, and also the foundation of a great bitterness. The poor White Man can live in the same land with the Negro only by insisting on a superiority due solely to his white skin. . . . Take away that mean dignity from the Poor White and he will at once assert his arrogance by means of the pogrom. Educators may preach and hope as they will, but the dictator of events is the populace. Between the Negro and the Poor White, as things stand, we see no possibility of compromise. And the higher the Negro climbs in the social scale, the more he brings the Poor White into disgrace, and the nearer he brings onto his own head a seemingly inevitable tragedy. Even as we write we note that during four months no case of lynching has occurred.

This is remarkable enough, but we have looked into the Poor White man's eye and do not feel optimistic. The future outbreak will be directed not against the Negro who has been tripped by his passions but against the one who would raise himself by his virtues.

Here in North Carolina conditions are better for the Negro than in Alabama, Georgia, or Mississippi. The wife of the head master told us, as a pleasing fact, that in the shops the clerks even address her as Mrs. The same was told us by the secretary of the coloured fair which we visited in the afternoon. He was even more delighted. "Why," he said, "there are people so nice in this town that they receive me in their houses like a friend and even allow me to eat with them, but of course in secret. Only they say, 'You must not feel hurt if we do not greet you in the street, we cannot flout prejudice as far as that.' "

And this man was so white, with fair straight hair and blue eyes, that we were astonished to hear him talking of himself as coloured.

V

THE GOSPEL OF JIM CROW

*They would have made Alexandre Dumas travel in
the Jim Crow car if he had come to Virginia. . . . They
even talk of "Jim Crow elevators" now in Southern
hotels.*

H. G. Wells, 1906

Jim Crow, an antebellum southern cartoon character of ill repute, became the slogan for the segregationist activities of the Democratic "Redeem-
ers" who controlled the ex-Confederate states after President Hayes's
compromise in 1877. Their rise to power coincided with their control of
the national House of Representatives beginning in 1874. Throughout the
1880s, most especially after the Supreme Court decision in 1883 outlaw-
ing the Civil Rights Act of 1875, jim-crow legislation superseded previously
established civil rights laws of the Reconstruction era. Racial demagoguery
was minimal until whites courted black political interests in the populist
movement of the early 1890s. As the competition between whites surfaced,
so did the exploitation of black electorates with the potential to upset any
political balance. Disfranchised blacks were more acceptable than blacks
voting for the wrong candidates. This development as well as America's
entrance into the affairs of international "colored" societies triggered the
rise of domestic racialistic movements at the turn of the century.

The gospel of jim crow reasoned that blacks were irresponsible and incapable of independence (Reconstruction failures were cited as examples).
The door was opened for the systematic removal of any legal rights. From
1890 to 1910 disfranchisement was successfully carried out by implemen-
tation of the grandfather clause, based on lineage; poll tax, an economic
factor; the literacy test, qualifying voters according to education; and the
Democratic white primary, which eliminated black participation. The
guarantees of the Fourteenth and Fifteenth Amendments were totally
disregarded and eliminated through legal loopholes in the laws.

Public segregation, in existence long before the Civil War, was developed
into a science in the post-Reconstruction era. A series of Supreme Court

decisions, culminating with Plessy vs. Ferguson (1896), opened the door for the total disregard of the rights of black citizens. "Separate but equal" was in reality separate and unequal. White men and ladies were accorded all public pleasures while black "boys" and "girls" were relegated to inferior facilities throughout the nation.

The white backlash, 1890–1920, developed from the fear and competition whites had of themselves and their relations with the "colored" world. Violence pervaded the country. Whites of all classes and ethnic groups, even non-English-speaking immigrant arrivals, participated in the folly of lynching blacks. Generally, when a region's economy faltered the result was often the castration and burning of a scapegoat black, selected by frustrated whites. The stereotypical black served the purpose well for the color-conscious whites.

Writers and movie producers brought a sense of professionalism to the antiblack surge. Thomas Dixon's *Leopard Spots* and *The Clansman* were highlights of racist literature. Bestial, mentally and culturally inferior blacks, particularly "apelike" men desirous of white women, romped through the pages of the nation's best-sellers. D. W. Griffith's *The Birth of a Nation* (1915) was acclaimed a motion picture success. The director's romantic portrayal of the rise of the Klan, based in part on Dixon's *The Clansman,* was a favorite of President Woodrow Wilson.

The rebirth of the KKK in 1915 signaled the final blow to blacks, already exposed to the organization's Reconstruction predecessor. The second Klan, a product of World War I and rural America's insecurities, was comprehensive in its hatred of blacks, Jews, Catholics, and foreigners. By 1923 an estimated 6,000,000 bona fide members swore allegiance to its program.

Some foreign travelers to the United States, reflecting their American contemporaries, joined in the "in thing" and condemned blacks.

WILLIAM LAIRD CLOWES

14: MISCEGENATION AND THE RACE
PROBLEM, 1890

Equality between the races is a hopeless dream;
yet the whole fabric of American institutions rests
upon the assumed equality of the citizens.

The subject of miscegenation fascinated foreigners, who marveled at
its "civilizing" effects on blacks. William Laird Clowes (1856–1905), English naval historian, writer, and reporter for *The Times* of London, was
commissioned in 1890 by that paper to do a story on race relations in the
southern United States. His letters, sent back to England, appeared between
November, 1890, and January, 1891. Clowes offered solutions to the
problems as well as commentary on the solutions offered by others. He
discounted black and white miscegenation as a solution. His ideas, however, do concur with contemporary racist myths propagandizing the
"purification" effects of white blood in blacks.

The United States have, both as individual States and as a Union, incurred towards the Negro liabilities which cannot be repudiated or shirked.
The country kidnapped and imported the Negro, enslaved him or connived
at his enslavement, used him for national purposes, freed him, and put power
into his hands; and it cannot now or ever shake off all responsibility concerning him. As he is, he is, for many reasons, an undesirable fellow-citizen; but
he was created a fellow-citizen to suit the temporary political interests of
the North; and, having served those interests, he is now to be disowned and
cast out a beggar. Equality between the races is a hopeless dream; yet the

William Laird Clowes, *Black America: A Study of the Ex-Slave and His Late Master*
(London, Cassell and Co., 1891), pp. 155–56, 165–67, 169–80.

whole fabric of American institutions rests upon the assumed equality of the citizens. If American institutions honestly and freely tolerated the existence of "classes," the race question would never have attained its present importance. The Negro, while "keeping his place," might still have enjoyed his vote. As things stand, he is practically, in spite of his nominal rights, an alien. When, as in the Reconstruction Period, he exercised his rights most fully, he did so to the prejudice of the rights of the Southern white, who was then, as it were, the alien. Now, when the white Southerner has fully resumed the exercise of his rights, the black man suffers proportionately. And every day's experience shows more and more clearly that real equality in the South, as between whites and blacks, is impossible of attainment.

Miscegenation is the most widely favoured and venerable of what I may call the quack nostrums for the cure of existing evils. The late Mr. Henry Woodfin Grady, one of the truest friends that the Negro ever had, laid it down as an axiomatic condition of harmony between races "that each race should earnestly desire a fusion of blood, in which all differences would be lost."

. . . .

Four centuries have not elapsed since the white man first set his foot on the eastern shore of the New World. Every step of his progress westward has been marked by the blood of the dissimilar race, which he found there and drove before him. He sits on the grave of the red man; he has shut the door in the face of the yellow man from China; what shall he do with the black man from Africa? Intermarry with him, say the quacks. But, to again quote Mr. Grady, "not only do the two races not earnestly desire fusion, but both races are pledged against it as the one impossible thing." This is quite notorious throughout the South, where it has even inspired legislation against miscegenation; yet many humanitarian theorists in the North still put forward intermarriage as the panacea.

. . . .

There are mulattoes in the United States, but nearly every mulatto is the offspring not of marriage but of an irregular, temporary, and disgraceful union. There are Eurasians in India, where, after all, whites and coloured people are racially related; yet even there most of the half-breeds are illegitimate. In Africa, in the meanwhile, the Hottentot and the Bushman, instead of blending with the whites, are vanishing. In Australia, too, and New Zealand, the aboriginal inhabitant is disappearing fast. Race, more than anything else, has to this day kept Central Africa a secret from the white world. And the numerical superiority of the Negroes in the Black Belt is, more than anything else, responsible for the fact that the Black Belt is almost a *terra incognita* to the mass of Northerners, and for the equally important fact

that European and Northern brains and capital do not go there as they go
to the whiter but not richer West. In the South, in the past five-and-twenty
years, the Negro has improved in very many respects; but that makes no
radical difference. He is still the Negro, and he always will be the Negro.

Yet in spite of these and other considerations that must be ever present
to the minds of all who know the South and are unprejudiced observers
of what is there for them to see, we find people persistently advocating
miscegenation as the certain cure for the evils of the situation. Mr. Frederick
Douglass, a mulatto, and, perhaps, the most distinguished coloured American now living, takes a somewhat neutral position. Writing in the *North
American Review* for May, 1886, on miscegenation, he says: "I am not a
propagandist, but a prophet. While I would not be understood as advocating
the desirability of such a result, I would not be understood as deprecating
it." But many whites have been bolder. The opinion of the Rev. B. T. Tanner is that "whether the whites and the blacks of the country shall mix is
no longer an open question, being settled by the fact that the mixing has
already, and to a large extent, taken place. . . . As we gaze," he continues,
"upon the millions of whites and millions of blacks confronting each other,
and as we remember that where there is no association there can be no
certain amity, and that where there is no amity there can be no lasting
peace, we are made to ask, What will the harvest be? As there cannot be
other than one Government, so there must not be ultimately more than
one people. The union of which we so justly boast must comprehend both."
And the language of Prof. S. B. Darnell, of the Cookman Institute, Jackson-
ville, is: "However we may feel on the subject, the stern logic of sequences
will make, in the coming years, 'our brother in black' a misnomer; and the
diverse streams of blood will so mingle that our posterity shall quote again,
'God hath made of one blood all nations of men.' "

. . . .

Between the races in America, as Judge Tourgée expresses it, "there
is no equalisation, no fraternity, no assimilation of rights, no reciprocity
of affection. Children may caress each other, because they are children.
Betwixt adults fewer demonstrations of affection are allowed than the
master bestows upon his dog. Ordinary politeness becomes a mark of shame.
A caress implies degradation. In all that region no man would stand in a
lady's presence unless uncovered. Yet not a white man in its borders dares
lift his hat to a coloured woman in the street, no matter how pure her life,
how noble her attributes, or how deep his obligations to her might be."

If such be the prevailing sentiments among Southern white people, the
questioner may say, How then do you account for the mulattoes, thousands
of whom are found in and far beyond the limits of the Black Belt? The
point is one concerning which I am anxious to convey a very clear understand-

ing, for it is a most important point. There is, undoubtedly, a large mixed population; and, as the Rev. Dr. B. T. Tanner has said, "the mixing has already taken place." It has taken place; it took place amid conditions which have ceased to exist; and practically it takes place no longer. It is in his assumption that the mixing process continues, and in his implied assumption that the causative unions were at any period and to any considerable extent legitimate ones, that Dr. Tanner creates a false impression.

The mulatto, strictly classified, is the offspring of a pure white and a pure black parent, and he is much less common than is generally supposed. In nine hundred and ninety-nine cases out of a thousand he is of illegitimate birth, and in ninety-nine cases out of a hundred, except, perhaps, in Louisiana, where there is a large population of French descent and of modified anti-Negro prejudices, he is a person no longer a minor. I made inquiries in Charleston with the object of discovering there a mulatto child of tender years, but in vain. I found mulattoes of five-and-twenty or thirty, but I could find no children. More than once in the street I thought that I had come upon what I was looking for; but in every case the child proved to be not a genuine mulatto, but simply a coloured child, the offspring, that is, of a parent or parents with some white blood, but not the direct offspring of black and white. The coloured people, as distinct from the pure-blooded Negroes, are everywhere common enough, and may be casually mistaken by the unfamiliar observer for mulattoes. But the real mulatto is comparatively rare, and is daily becoming rarer. Most of the coloured people have less than one-half white blood; an overwhelming majority, indeed, have less than one-quarter. A coloured person with but one-eighth or one-sixteenth of Negro blood is very rare indeed. The kind of proportion that is common is ten-twelfths or fourteen-sixteenths, or even more. All this points to the fact that miscegenation, although at one time prevalent, has, as I have said, practically ceased.

The truth is that the mulatto, the quadroon, and the octoroon are chiefly products of the slavery period. Since the war, the birth of a mulatto, quadroon, or octoroon out of wedlock has been of the rarest occurrence; and legislation and prejudice have limited, and well-nigh put a stop to, the birth of these people in wedlock. Mulattoes intermarry, and, in some cases, have intermarried for generations. In more than one place in the South they, with occasional admixture of quadroons, constitute a small, distinct community of highly respectable people, living to themselves for the most part, and having as little in common with their black as with their white neighbours; for white blood, even in small quantities, "tells," and the pride of the mulatto or quadroon, as a rule, rebels as much at the idea of alliance with the Negro as does the pride of the white at the idea of alliance with coloured or black. The mulatto originated in the desire of the slave woman to enjoy the favour of her white master, and in the desire of the master to add to his possessions—as well as, to some extent, in white brutality and youthful dissoluteness, at a period when these could be very freely indulged. The black slave woman and the white master have disappeared, and all the conditions have changed. With the changed conditions the birth of mulattoes, of quadroons, and of octoroons has steadily grown rarer and rarer, until it threatens to cease altogether. If miscegenation ever promised to solve the Negro problem—and this I doubt—emancipation hopelessly destroyed the prospect. Whatever miscegenation there was, was entirely confined to white men and Negro or coloured women. The Southern white woman has had no part in it. In her opinion it is, in all circumstances and conditions, loathsome and abominable. Miscegenation, upon the only principles in accordance with which it has ever been practised between the races in the United States, is, after all, no real miscegenation at all. It was one-sided, it was criminal, it involved the disowning of the child by the stronger of its parents. Could any satisfactory admixture have been effected on such terms? And there has never been the slightest sign of assimilation on any other terms.

There is yet another aspect of the question, and that is, Is the mulatto, the quadroon, the octoroon, a desirable product? It cannot be denied that the intelligence, the general aptitude for affairs, the business and political capacity, the aesthetic faculty, and the finer qualities of the coloured man, are always closely proportionate to the degree of whiteness of his skin. In the coloured man we continually find a perception of artistic beauty in form, colour, and effect, and what may be called a natural sense of decency and shame. These are foreign to the Negro nature; and their peculiar absence seems to widen the already sufficiently broad gulf between pure black and pure white. In the coloured man, again, we find the natural leader of the Negro in all movements, political, religious, and social. The only representative of the coloured population who ever sat in the United States Senate was nearly white; and in the Reconstruction period the masters of the situation in the South were, not Northern whites and Southern Negroes, but Northern whites and Southern coloured men. The hybrid of the white man's begetting was then the white man's scourge. Beyond a doubt, he is intellectually a great improvement upon the black. But he is no nearer the white than was his black mother. "If," says the author of "An appeal to Pharaoh," "the Negro race were wholly supplanted on American soil by a race of mulattoes, or even of octoroons, the race problem would be so far from approaching a solution, that it would be at least as perplexing and as fraught with present difficulty and promise of future trouble as is the Negro problem of to-day." And, apart from this, the mulatto is physically and constitutionally, and also to, I fear, a very large extent, morally, a failure. Although both white and Negro are long-lived races, the mulatto, born of Anglo-Saxon and Negro, very rarely attains the age of fifty; and he is particularly and abnormally subject to certain forms of disease. Moreover, there is a general and, I believe, a not unfounded impression that nature refuses to perpetuate beyond two or three generations this race of human hybrids. Dr. J. C. Knott, after nearly fifty years of residence among the black and white races of the South, declared mulattoes to be "the shortest-lived of any class of the human family," and that the product of the cross between the Anglo-Saxon and the Negro dies off before the dark stain can be washed out by amalgamation; while Professor Drummond says, "Inappropriate hybridism is checked by the law of sterility." This last doctrine may, it is just possible, not apply, or may only apply to a limited extent, to the mulatto. There is, unfortunately, less room for doubt that, in the South, people of mixed blood furnish a surprisingly and disproportionately large quota to the criminal population. It was estimated that in the Mississippi Penitentiary, on the 1st of December, 1885, there was one white for every 4,480 white inhabitants of the State, one black for every 918 black inhabitants, and one "coloured" for every 314 "coloured" inhabitants. I am not desirous of asking too much attention to this particular estimate, which is open to error, for the reason that, in the census reports, black and "coloured" people are classed together; but I feel bound to say that, upon showing this estimate to the superintendents of several convict establishments in the South, I have been invariably told that, whether exact or inexact, it might be accepted as expressive of the general truth. If, therefore, the products of miscegenation be short life and excessive tendency to disease and crime, is miscegenation, even supposing honourable and legal miscegenation to be possible, a desirable way out of the difficulty? I venture to think not. Honourable miscengenation, besides, is out of the question.

15: ANTIBLACK THOUGHT, 1900-14

*To the enemies of the Negro race it has been
sarcastically observed, "Why not rather despatch
them all off at once to Mars, or some other planet?"*

Abbé Félix Klein (1862-1954), a French Catholic priest, visited the
United States just after the turn of the century. His report, *In the Land
of the Strenuous Life,* originally published in 1904, criticizes the jim crow
practices of the era, including the "deplorable" colonization scheme. Klein
praised the efforts of Booker T. Washington and the Tuskegee "machine."

To see these 530 young Negroes and Negresses, well dressed and well
bred, under teachers of their own race, pursuing the same studies as our
average college students, who would dream of the existence of a terrible
race-question in the United States? I have said elsewhere that the conflict
between the various nationalities in the Republic possesses real seriousness
only in the fervid imagination of Europeans. But it is not so with the antagonism between the whites and the blacks, or rather with the difficulty of
making two peoples, the most widely different that can be imagined, live
side by side: the Americans—the most modern and progressive of men; and
the Negroes—primitive and rudimentary beings repressed and kept down to
the lowest degree of evolution by three centuries of slavery and thousands
of years spent in savagery.

Socially, the white man experiences a strong repugnance to the society
of Negroes; and the latter, especially when they are numerous, as in the

Abbé Félix Klein, *In the Land of the Strenuous Life* (Chicago, A. C. McClurg and
Co., 1905), pp. 296-303.

South, are obliged to have their own schools and churches, their own places of meeting, and special reserved places in cars and omnibuses. To admit them to one's table would be considered scandalous; and the act of President Roosevelt, though without significance to us, in inviting Booker T. Washington to dine with him at the White House, was regarded with abhorrence by prominent newspapers of the South.

Morally, the Negroes are reproached for their tendency to thievishness, laziness, and vanity, but above all, for such a shocking lack of respect for white women that the latter in some places are subject to continual alarm; and it is usually for this offence, be it said without any wish to justify the custom, that the odious practice of lynching has sprung up. Professor W. E. B. Du Bois, an eminent professor in the colored University of Atlanta, and himself a Negro, says that out of every hundred of his race nine are hopelessly vicious, ten intelligent, and the rest more or less destitute of resources, of education, or of true independence.

Politically, the Negroes enjoy the same rights as the white men; they have sometimes controlled elections, and there are States where in a not far distant future they may be able to secure a majority and thus make themselves masters of the situation. Can one picture Americans submitting to a government by blacks? Up to the present time, clever laws, adroit manoeuvres, and, it must be said, election frauds also, have averted this peril, this "defeat of civilization." But in this matter there are limits of which the inviolable Constitution prohibits the transgression; and, moreover, the difficulty cannot always be got rid of by making electoral ballots good for admission to a circus, by so multiplying the ballot-boxes that the ignorant cannot tell where to cast a vote, or, as in Louisiana, by requiring all native-born citizens to pay a voting tax of three hundred dollars unless their ancestors possessed the right to vote before 1862, the year of emancipation for the blacks.

In all this there is hardly any danger for the North, protected as it is by its climate; the Negroes there are less numerous, and their cause rather excites sympathy. In the central regions, where one sees a large number of them, they are less esteemed, but not yet feared. It is in the South that people are uneasy and irritated, that they seek means to avoid the growing "peril," and that they propose solutions not one of which seems to be acceptable to the good sense, the fairness, the Christian spirit, and the sentiment of justice which, thank God! prevail among the majority of the citizens.

No one of any intelligence speaks seriously of exterminating the Negroes, or of returning them to slavery. Very few hope, even in a remote future, for the fusion of the races: cases of marriage between whites and blacks are very exceptional, and there are States in the South where such marriages are prohibited by law; it is asserted, moreover, that with the mixed race fecundity ceases after two or three generations. Others, a little more numerous, propose the absolute separation of the races by the removal of the Negroes; it would only be necessary, they say, to send them back to Africa, or to the Philippines, or to reserve a State for them exclusively— for example, southern California. If it is too complicated a matter to send them all away at one swoop (they are nearly ten millions in number), let 125,000 of their women be expatriated every year. The whole transaction would cost hardly $400,000. This would not be paying too dearly for the future welfare of the nation, and for the removal from the path of the Anglo-Saxon of an obstacle which may compromise his high destiny. Needless to say, up to the present at least, good men, and in fact all men of sound judgment, refuse to consider a project so impracticable and so obnoxious to the Negroes, who do not find themselves at all badly off in the United States, and would not, it is safe to say, leave the country unless constrained by violence to do so. To the enemies of the Negro race it has been sarcastically observed, "Why not rather despatch them all off at once to Mars, or some other planet?" The good conduct of the black regiments in the Spanish-American war cannot be forgotten, and the question is asked if they have not the right to live in a country after having voluntarily risked their lives for it.

But it is easier to discard a poor solution than to find a good one, and I must say that not one of the many eminent men with whom I discussed this problem of the Negro can perceive any real way out of the difficulty. They understand, indeed, that they are in this predicament by reason of the crime that was committed in stealing the blacks out of their own country, the mistake that was perhaps made in emancipating them without preparation, and certainly in conferring upon them at the outset full political rights; but how now to redeem these errors, without violating the sacred principles of the Constitution, is the problem. It would be well to raise the franchise qualifications; but that would remedy only a small number of inconveniences, and it should, to be just, apply to the whites as well as to the Negroes; it is hardly likely that the whites will allow themselves to be deprived of their acquired power. Must we, then, give way to alarm and discouragement? That would not be American. As it stands, the situation is still tolerable; if in the future it should become more serious, we shall then discover a way to remedy it. Is not the United States able to fight its own battles? And, any way, what is the use of borrowing trouble?

We recognize in this the invincible optimism of a people conscious of their vitality. But although it may help us to bear them better, confidence in the future is not a direct remedy for present evils; it is not solving the

Negro problem to say that it will end by solving itself. Therefore, the most discerning minds and the most generous souls are devoting themselves with all their strength to the education of the blacks, the only work which is at present good, and the only one from which we may expect, in default of a prompt and universal regeneration of the race, at least the certain material and moral amelioration of a considerable number.

But what education will be the most efficacious? Frankly, I do not believe it will be that of which we saw so brilliant an example in the high school. Higher education is necessary for the Negroes, to train up among them teachers, doctors, lawyers, ministers—a picked class able to assure leadership, and to aid their rise toward a better life. But such education must be only by way of exception, if it is not to result in the formation of a lot of second-rate leaders unfitted for serious work. What the great majority need in the way of education is, together with the reading, writing, and arithmetic, a practical and technical training, a preparation for business, and, better yet, for the manual trades.

It is with this idea in mind that the admirable Booker T. Washington is training the eleven hundred pupils in his institute at Tuskegee, where young girls are taught housekeeping as well as bookkeeping, and household science with more care than the science of history; where the young men themselves have built the school and manufactured the furniture of their rooms; where two days out of every five are devoted to work that was once, but is not now, called servile. "I believe in the future of my race," says this great educator, [*Up from Slavery*] "in proportion as they learn to do better than anybody else does, and as they learn how to render services which shall be regarded as indispensable." And he cites as an example his own experience at the Hampton School, where he was employed as a porter and given the privilege of attending the lectures because he had swept to perfection the rooms assigned him to do the first day. The Negroes can clean better than others; they can become excellent workmen in all kinds of trades; at Tuskegee they make bricks whose reputation for excellence has spread abroad, and which find a ready market in the neighborhood; but many years and perhaps many centuries must pass before they can discharge "better than anybody else" the social duties of a superior race. Their great liberator, Abraham Lincoln, was a manual laborer before he became President of the United States. Races follow the same process of evolution as individuals, only much more slowly.

Pascal considers "all mankind in the course of ages as one man who exists forever and who is continually learning." But it is not forty years since the mass of Negroes in America began "to learn." The progress they have made in that short period leaves them still a long way behind the other citizens of the Republic, and it is from this fact that the grave difficulties of the question arise; but the ground covered is appreciable, and we can to some extent agree with this view of Booker T. Washington himself: "One must have been in contact with the Negroes for twenty years, as I have been, in the very heart of the South, to appreciate the fact that they are doing well, in spite of all that can be said; developing slowly, perhaps, but surely, whether from the material, the moral, or the intellectual point of view." To-day, no doubt, sixty out of every hundred Negroes remain illiterate; but it is not half a century since they were nearly all so, and since the laws of many States, as, for example, Louisiana and North Carolina, punished with a fine of two hundred dollars the shocking crime of attempting to teach them to read. Even the poorest Negro homes in the cities of America to-day are like royal palaces compared with the old-time cabin of "Uncle Tom" and the African hut which for countless centuries sheltered so many generations of savage life.

MAURICE SMETHURST EVANS

16: SOUTH AFRICAN VIEWS OF AMERICAN RACISM, 1915

*. . . A Negro had been done to death by a white
mob for preaching colonization to Africa.*

The Englishman Maurice Smethurst Evans (1854–1920) moved to South
Africa in 1875, where he later served in that country's Legislative Assembly.
He spent much of his life studying black-white race relations in Africa, and
just before World War I he visited the United States to investigate the
black situation and compare it with conditions in his land. Most of his
impressions were made while in the southern states. Evans believed that
the race problem in the United States was in part agitated by whites.
White racism permeated most levels of the society he toured. The following selection from his American study explores the jim crow mind.

Sitting one day on a barrel in a country store, having been introduced
by a local man as an African, I was asked by one of those present whether
the Negroes they had in the South were real Negroes or not. He said he
had been told by one who claimed special knowledge on the subject, that
the real African Negro had a tail about four inches long and did not possess
a soul. Was this so?
Another guessed that they had a powerful lot of Negroes in North
Carolina; more niggers he reckoned than there were in all Africa.

Maurice Smethurst Evans, *Black and White in the Southern States: A Study of the
Race Problem in the United States from a South African Point of View* (London
and New York, Longmans, Green and Co., 1915), pp. 60–61, 65–69, 77–81.

Judged by the standard of Britain and the British Colonies, the Southern white man cannot be regarded as a law-abiding person. Homicide is a weakness peculiar to him. Few newspapers are issued without a report of shooting, wounding, and killing. And this seems to be lightly regarded. Although I never actually saw shooting going on, once or twice I was in the neighbourhood of gunplay, and heard the current remarks thereon. It was in each case between white men. The facts were stated by witnesses in an indifferent way, as casually as if they were speaking of an unavoidable accident. This indifference would have been still more marked had the victim been a Negro. Had it, however, been a case of black shooting white, I saw and heard sufficient to make me feel that the attitude would have been quite different. Then one might expect race riot and lynching, and the actual perpetrator would not be the only one to suffer. In the case of white shooters, whether the victim be white or black, adequate punishment, according to our ideas, is seldom inflicted. Juries seem to regard the crime lightly, and even when punishment is incurred, the friends of the criminal often bring pressure to bear on the authorities and he is released. I have heard several theories given to account for this phenomenon, but none seems to me to fully account for it. The presence of a subservient race who may be imposed upon with comparative impunity, does certainly lead to an arrogant and masterful attitude on the part of the stronger race. The popular election of those who administer the law, and the absence of rural police must also be taken into account. The common practice of carrying weapons in many sections is alleged as a cause, and of course no shooting could happen if there were no guns. But we in South Africa are accustomed to firearms, have during the past forty years used them in legitimate warfare far oftener than the Southern people, and yet homicide is not a favourite pastime with either Dutch or English. And if murder does happen, we are content to let the law take its course, we do not desire personally to kill the offender. . . .

All through the South one sees evidence of religious observance. . . . In the towns churches are numerous, and often large and well built in proportion to the population. In the country one passes little frame churches at frequent intervals. . . . I attended many Church services, mostly of those belonging to denominations holding Evangelical views, which form the majority in the South. . . . The attendance was generally good, with a great proportion of women, but with a larger number of men than one usually sees in England and the Colonies in these days. Once when attending such a service and looking round at the staid and devout worshippers, I remembered the facts of a lynching that had taken place in the neighbourhood, and could not help wondering whether any of those I saw with bowed heads had been present, and what their views on such an occurrence would be. I felt the discords and antagonisms that everywhere go to make up our human nature. But the contrast is not often so forcibly brought home to one. I never saw a Negro in these churches, they have their separate organizations, managed entirely by themselves. . . .

Before Emancipation the white churches in the South supported the institution of slavery, and numerous clerical writers could be cited who attempted to prove from Scripture that it was of Divine origin and had the Divine sanction. To-day there are their descendants, Christian ministers who condone if they do not approve lynching, and who turn to the Scripture to prove that the Negro is, and always will be, an inferior, and attempt thus to justify discrimination and repression. To the Negrophilist and humanitarian of Western Europe this sounds the rankest hypocrisy. But the Southerner is not the only man who clips his religion to suit his peculiar sins and environment.

Just as in South Africa no general conversation touching on public affairs can be long continued without bringing in the native, so in the South the Negro is never far below the surface in the minds and conversation of all one meets. Should the topic of conversation be agriculture, Negro labour and Negro tenants crop up; if it is skilled labour and its organization, the question of the admittance of the Negro comes forward; should it be social betterment in cities, then the problem of the Negro dives and tenderloin districts is included; if it is the prohibition question, again the Negro and how he affects it. Direct questions on the part of the investigator are not necessary to bring up this topic; it is near to the top in the minds of all, and a little tact will elicit opinion and attitude. I found a firmly fixed, inexorable belief in the racial inferiority of the Negro possessed the minds of most, and opinion varied from a contemptuous tolerance to an out-spoken hostility. A nigger must be kept in his place, and that place was a subordinate one, industrially, politically, and especially socially. A watchful suspicion on all attempts which could be interpreted as claiming equality was almost universal. It was expressed most strongly on two phases, a fear that the Negro would impinge on their source of livelihood, and a dread that he would attempt to claim social equality, which implied to them the destruction of race integrity. On these two foundations was based the great mass of animosity, and it expressed itself in many practical ways, some similar to those we observe in South Africa, others somewhat different and curiously different. For instance, in South Africa the average white man never shakes hands with a native, excepting perhaps on occasion when he has something to gain, and then with a qualm, or it may be in the native territories and with a chief. In the South there does not seem to be the same objection to this act of courtesy, though it is not common. There seems, however, to be the strongest distaste to prefix Mr. or Mrs. to the name of a Negro or Negress. One Negro writer, in speaking of the contemptuous attitude of Southern men to coloured women, states he has never known a white man to use this politeness to a coloured woman. Many of those I spoke to when asked as to the condition of the Negroes in their section would reply they were in good shape now, but some little time ago they got "bigotty"; shooting had however occurred, they had received a lesson, and all was well now. Several on different occasions expressed the opinion that at intervals, more or less frequent, it was necessary to give the niggers a lesson. Reference was often made to some outstanding occasion, such as the Atlanta race riots, which had been conspicuously successful in putting the nigger in his place, and men present at these scenes of violence often volunteered the information that on such occasions the casualties were greater than reported. I often wondered what would happen to a Negrophilist who used the usual arguments about race equality if he began talking in a public place to these quiet, watchful, determined-looking men. I never ventured the experiment. I simply listened and questioned.

While I was in the South the first ordinances were being passed to prevent the races occupying the same sections in Southern cities—Baltimore taking the lead. Hitherto the Negro has been practically segregated in the lowest quarters; now the comparatively well-to-do naturally want better surroundings and have bought or rented houses in white neighbourhoods, and caused much resentment, and undoubtedly in some cases depreciation in the value of the adjacent property held and occupied by the whites. This is a condition of things bound to come as increasing numbers of Negroes desire a better environment, and it is responded to on the part of the whites by Segregation Ordinances. The example of Baltimore has been followed by many other cities, and legislation to effect this purpose has been introduced in several Southern States, backed apparently by a popular determination to bring the matter to an issue.

There are quite a number of coloured male and female clerks employed in the public service. In proportion to the total Negro population the percentage so employed is very small, but in Washington, D. C., there are quite a respectable number employed in the various offices. There has recently been a deliberate and sustained effort to draw distinctions, devised to separate the white and black clerks beyond anything hitherto attempted. This has been controversially dealt with in some of the newspapers, and organized efforts have been made by the coloured people and their friends to defeat it. They may or may not succeed. The significant fact for us is that such attempts are possible, and are constantly being made to-day in many directions, entailing constant vigilance on the part of those whom they affect.

Serious attempts have been made of late to limit the State appropriations to Negro education. There seems to have been a recrudescence of opposition to the literary education of the black man, as unfitting him for his proper sphere. I met the principal of a State Normal Coloured School in the South who told me he had only just secured his annual appropriation by the most persistent and energetic lobbying, and others informed me that it would never have been obtained but for this special effort, and the personal respect of the Legislature for the principal. There have of course been times of violent opposition to Negro education in the past; it is nothing new. It is a burning question and sometimes the opposition blazes forth, again smoulders, or is quiescent. I cannot pretend to determine whether the present hostility is simply a temporary set-back, marking a passing phase, or not. It has, however, been causing some present anxiety to those who ᴧ are friendly to better education, and seems to signify, with other tendencies, a disposition in some quarters towards renewed criticism of the value of, at least, *higher* literary education for the Negro.

Concurrently with this disposition to curtail opportunity there has been a movement to introduce legislation to prevent any white person from teaching in a coloured school. This is a distinct innovation, for hitherto much of the higher Negro education in the South has been in the hands of white organizers and teachers from the North. It is true that such teachers have been viewed with disfavour by the whole South, and social ostracism has often been their portion, but there has hitherto been no law to prevent it.

Now I must state a paradox, but one which will be understood by South Africans. Many Southerners told me that the Negro was an incubus on the South, that he held back the true progress of the country, and that his presence had demoralized their people: and yet—they could not do without him.

The most virulent nigger haters would often be the first to resent bitterly any attempt to remove him. Through his labour and by reason of his submissive disposition, their lives are made easy for them, and while acutely jealous of any attempt on his part to advance, they will not let him go.

One Southern writer says: "I know of several counties, not a hundred miles from Atlanta, where it is more than a man's life is worth to go in and get Negroes to move to another State. There are farmers who would not hesitate to shoot their own brother were he to come in from Mississippi to get 'his niggers' as he calls them, even if he had no contract with them.". . .

I was told by a very intelligent mulatto I met in Alabama that in the neighborhood in which he lived a Negro had been done to death by a white mob for preaching colonization to Africa.

Summing up the general position in the most conservative way, I would say that in the South, while race prejudice generally, and repression and

differentiation in particular, may not be actually growing in intensity, it
is in some respects changing, and it is certainly not decreasing. Among
the mass of the people it is intensely bitter, and liable at any moment, and
for causes that seem entirely inadequate, to break out in active hostility,
race riots, shooting, and lynching. At best it is a banked fire; a sweep of
suspicion and flame breaks out.

I have tried to give my impressions of the feelings of the average Southerner towards the Negro, without bias. It is essential that it should be understood. It is painful to have to record that a people of our own race should
be so saturated with hostility to a weaker one, which is unable to defend
itself, either at law, or by force of arms.

We have race prejudice and to spare in South Africa. It is very difficult
for anyone, however experienced and impartial, to correctly assess the
comparative depth and intensity of this feeling in the two countries. My
impression is, however, that we are more tolerant and well disposed towards
the native, as we are certainly more law-respecting in our relations to him,
than are the people of the South. What is happening there of subversion
of right and justice with its maleficent reflex action on character should,
I think, act as a warning to us to keep a close watch and firm hand on
any tendency to exaggerated prejudice.

The Negro people of the South are but one-third of the total population.
Ours in South Africa is overwhelmingly preponderant. Increase of our
white population has been urged as a possible solution of the native problem. In the light of the experience of the United States it does not appear
probable that any possible readjustment of the relative numbers of the
two races in South Africa would necessarily have this result. We must still
patiently study, we must still watch and wait; the problem will still be
with us.

This chapter would sound hopeless enough if this was all. Thank God
it is not. Even in the old, bad slave days there were Southerners who could
think straight, and act justly. Some such, convinced of the unrighteousness
of holding their fellow-man in bonds, set free their slaves and reduced
themselves to penury, and their deeds do follow them. I had the privilege
of meeting Southern men and women of tender conscience and high ideals
who deplored the common attitude, and who I know dealt justly and kindly
in all their relations with the weaker race. And such are not altogether isolated. They have begun to band themselves together to work for improved
conditions, and to strive for the betterment of the Negro people. Great
courage and infinite tact and judgment are required, and these are in
evidence.

At the first Southern Sociological Congress held at Nashville, Tenn.,
at which I was present, there was a special section to study and discuss

Negro questions, and the opinion of the better South was there reflected. Negroes were present at the discussions and freely joined in them. Reports were given of social work done among the Negro population by Southern organizations. Among others was an association of men from the various Southern Universities, formed with the special object of accurately studying the social relations of the races and working for betterment. It was also announced, to the surprise of some at a distance to whom I told it, that cooperation between the white girl students of the High School and the coloured girl students of Fisk University was in contemplation, to work to improve the position and life of Negro women and children in the city.

I attended this Congress as I was going North, and after an experience of the Black Belt, and an almost undiluted diet of the ordinary Southern talk on the nigger, his weaknesses and inordinate pretensions, and the necessity for keeping him in check, the sane and liberal tone in these discussions came as a hopeful and welcome change.

VI

URBANIZATION

> *The Negro . . . more than the men of any other race,*
> *lives in such an intimate communion with nature,*
> *that he seems more capable than other men of shud-*
> *dering and rejoicing with her changes.*
>
> José Martí, 1886

Blacks have lived in American cities since the first colonial settlements established in Virginia. Their numbers increased greatly after the Civil War, during which time they were attracted by available jobs, fear of rural white lynch mobs, and the possibility of escape from the fiascos of sharecropping. Migration to the North began in the 1890s, reaching peaks during both World War I and II. The Great Migration (1914–30) is one of the largest domestic population movements in American history, with an estimated 1,500,000 people having moved into Chicago, St. Louis, Detroit, Cleveland, Baltimore, Philadelphia, New York, and Newark, among other cities. Major developments in the North and South provide the backdrop for this mass exodus.

The movement of southern blacks during Reconstruction, essentially an intraregional phenomenon, resulted from the diminished hopes of Republicans threatened after their party's demise in the up-country districts. The subsequent Compromise of 1877 all but left southern blacks at the mercy of the Redeemer governments. The failure of land reform, rise of debts, disfranchisement of the already restricted black electorates in the 1890s, and the competition from poor whites tightened the noose and lessened any chances for mass black development in the late nineteenth-century South. Economic fortunes further declined during the infestation of the Mexican boll weevil, which destroyed thousands of acres of cotton farms. There were few reasons for most black folk to stay in the South. Opportunity had only to call.

Northern industrial expansion and labor-management conflicts in the factories in the years 1890 to 1920 provided the chance blacks had been awaiting for so long. Companies advertised in black newspapers, hoping to lure southern rural workers into the low-wage positions now available because of expansion and striking white employees. The response was immediate: blacks loaded onto the trains headed north. Ghettoes were overcome by the additional burden of thousands of homeless, jobless migrants.

The new arrivals were not welcomed with open arms. Sometimes not even expected jobs were there. Most unions remained segregated, thereby forcing blacks to become scabs. White resentment turned to anger and violence, especially during the war years 1914-19 and 1941-45.

Life in the inner cities was rough, in part because of the unhealthy conditions of poor housing, filth, and pollution. Tuberculosis became a major killer of blacks. The winters were cold, with little or no heating; the summers were hot, with little promise of escape from the heat and stench of industry. Apartments, too large and expensive for the migrant families, were advertised for additional boarders.

Ghetto life seriously jeopardized family stability. Male unemployment often surpassed female levels, and in turn marital relationships were strained in the male-dominated society. Black women were more likely to get a wage, though the quality of work usually remained on the domestic scale. This was foreign to rural people accustomed to the familial nature of sharecropping and tenant farming. The nature of residential arrangements was just as unfortunate. The once standard extended family under the same roof or in close proximity became a memory. In the North as children got older they moved to other sections of town, sometimes miles away. Togetherness was difficult to maintain with this family dispersion.

Black communities were transformed into poverty-stricken ghettoes where services decayed and get-rich landlords charged exorbitant rents to blacks who would otherwise have no other places to stay.

ANDRÉ SIEGFRIED

17: JIM CROW LAWS AND BLACK MIGRATION, 1920s

*There is a great gulf between the civilized Negro of
Harlem and the husky brute of the Mississippi
plantation. . . .*

André Siegfried (1875–1959), French economist, historian, journalist,
and professor of economic geography at École des Sciences Politiques,
Paris, and later at the Collège de France, visited the United States in 1898
and again in the mid 1920s. He wrote numerous books, including *America
Comes of Age* (1927). In this study Siegfried elaborates on jim-crow policy
and the migration of blacks to the cities of the North and Midwest. The
author's analysis of the Afro-American condition is disturbing.

The Americans have inherited from the English a horror of intermarriage between white and coloured people that is little less than fanatic,
and therefore the existence of ten and a half million blacks within the country
creates an insoluble problem before which even the stoutest must quail.
After the Civil War the victorious Northerners imagined that they could
solve the Negro question by suppressing slavery, but the race hatred that
has since resulted is much worse. Slavery in a sense was a solution, for it
established a definite hierarchy, in contrast to the present brutal domina-
tion of one race over the other, which is maintained by a system of intimidation without any regard to the law. The North may have thought that

André Siegfried, *America Comes of Age: A French Analysis,* translated by H. H.
Hemming and Doris Hemming (New York, Harcourt, Brace, 1927), pp. 91–96, 100–
108. Reprinted by permission of the executors of the Siegfried estate, the translators,
and Jonathan Cape Ltd.

it had imposed its point of view, but the South has undoubtedly had the last word.

. . . .

If we are to believe the Southerners, the whole question has been settled, and there is no longer a Negro problem—or at any rate, if there is one it is entirely a local matter which they are capable of managing without interference from the country. The Negro, they say, is acknowledged to be an inferior race that has been degraded by slavery and is not susceptible to education. He must be ruthlessly kept at the bottom of the ladder as God intended, and it is absolutely impious to try to alter him. It is only at this level that he can be useful to the community, and so long as he is content to remain there forever without trying to rise, they will admit that they are very fond of him individually and that he has great charm. Through years of living side by side they have learned to understand him. They know how to talk to him, how to make him work, how to joke with him and yet keep him in his place. He is a child, and they treat him as such and protect him because it is their duty. Properly handled, he is easy to manage, but give him authority and he becomes a dangerous brute that must be crushed. It is not a question of sentiment—and this is important—nor yet of ethics and morals, but of prestige, and even of the very existence of the white race. The South has always been a white man's country, and they intend to keep it so; if necessary, at the point of the sword. Busy-bodies in the North who stir up the darkies by talking to them of their dignity and their rights neither know them nor like them—"so for heaven's sake," they say, "leave us alone, for we know what we are doing."

This argument, which is repeated again and again, throws a clear light on the undercurrent of thought in the southern mind. Their selfish good humour is mixed with the paternalism of the master who will never admit that the servant can become his equal and is ferociously jealous lest the latter should try to improve his position. They will resort to anything to keep him in his place—violence, massacre, and even torture. . . .

By the "Jim Crow laws," which are rigidly applied, the southern Negroes are ordered to travel in separate coaches, and to sit only in the back of the trams. These laws go even further and reserve certain quarters of the towns for the whites, and forbid the blacks either to rent or buy houses there. There are whole counties which the blacks may not enter, and they cannot even leave the trains passing through. Such legislation is almost superfluous, since the whites take it on themselves to apply these rules whether they are legal or not. A Negro was once lynched by a furious mob in a theatre, because he dared to sit down in the part reserved for the whites. A complete "sanitary cordon" has been established, which even includes the churches. In the South the majority of both races are Baptists or Methodists, but their churches are always separate; so they do not even pray together. Humiliation extends to the most trivial details of daily life. No matter who he may be, the Negro must go into a house by the back door; for no white servant would allow him to enter otherwise. He is never addressed as "Mister," be he a bishop or a doctor, but simply as John or Joseph. Sometimes, if they wish to be especially polite, they call him "Professor," an appellation to which a certain amount of irony is attached in English, I have noticed.

Against such oppression, which at times amounts to persecution, the black man is helpless. He has no political representation and has no way of airing his grievances. Also it is difficult for him to obtain justice, for the two races are by no means on an equal footing in the courts. The statements of the whites are always accepted until they are proved to be false, but a coloured man must produce ten times as much evidence. The southern administration makes no attempt to conceal such injustices. In the matter of education, for example, the black population is deliberately kept in a state of inferiority. In South Carolina the Negroes number 51 per cent. of the population, but their share of the education funds amounts to only 11 per cent. The whites do not wish them to progress, for they need them to supply the lowest type of manual labour.

We find the same injustice in municipal administration, for the blacks are relegated to the unhealthy and badly-kept parts of the towns, and all the money is spent on the quarters reserved for the whites. In the part that belongs to the privileged race the streets are swept; there are pavements, gutters, and arc lights; but two hundred yards away the Negroes live in hovels with cesspools instead of sewers, and total darkness in their streets at night. In 1922 the death rate in the southern cities was 12.1 per 1,000 whites, but 20.5 among the blacks. How often have I heard these figures commented upon with a grim smile—"Tuberculosis and pneumonia may perhaps be the solution of the problem, and may save us from being overrun by these creatures."

The Southerners can exploit these illiterate masses with complete impunity, since there is no court of appeal where they can receive justice. Only a short while ago it was quite common for them to take advantage of the small coloured farmer in the country districts. They deceived him about the exact area of his farm, and when he had to pay his rent in kind, they gave him very little say as to what he had produced, even dictating the amount of his payment to him. His final reckoning was indefinitely delayed, and in the end he was forced to accept it, whether correct or otherwise. Such conditions no longer exist to the same extent, for war-time prosperity has even reached the small black proprietors, and in addition the wholesale immigration of the Negroes to the northern cities has at last made the southern employers reflect. But the economic contest between the races is not carried on with equal weapons, for not only must the Negro win the good will of the employers, but what is far more difficult, he must also overcome the ferocious jealousy of the "poor white" class, who are the bitterest enemies of his race. . . .

In the South, at any rate, the Negroes have passively resigned themselves to existing conditions. Their attitude is that of parasites, gravitating around the whites, whom they consider their patrons. The title "Boss," which they often use for the whites, reflects their instinctive recognition of their ethnic position, and when they classify themselves into their own social categories, their viewpoint is much the same. To be the descendant of a slave is humiliating. At Charleston, Richmond, etc., certain groups from the West Indies whose ancestors were free are regarded as superior, and therefore they do not mix with the others. By much the same snobbery that we find among the domestics of old British families, it is considered the thing to be descended from the slaves who belonged to one of the first families of Virginia. Therefore it is not astonishing that a relatively fair skin is appreciated by the Negroes themselves. They distinguish all sorts of shades of colour which escape us—black, brown, deep brown, yellow, reddish brown, deep yellow, dark brown, chocolate, gingerbread, fair, light brown, red, pink, tan, olive, copper colour, blue, cream, pale black, dead black, bronze, banana. . . . Pale complexions, are more frequently met with in North Carolina and Virginia than in the extreme South. It is interesting to note that in the smart Negro churches the best pews are reserved for the palest of the faithful. On the contrary, among the lower classes of Negro the really black man inspires greater confidence, an observation which applies, for example, to the minister of a low-class Baptist community, whose colour renders disloyalty to his race impossible. Coloured people actually exist whose tint is so pale that they can be mistaken for whites. They can "pass" (a sacred expression among the Negroes); that is to say, they move undetected into the superior race, where they are lost.

With the possible exception of a small *élite,* humility is the dominant trait of the southern Negroes. They are docile, passive, and accept their subjugation without a murmur. A Spartacist revolt is the last thing to be feared, for their efforts are directed rather toward adaptation. Circumstances have developed in them an extraordinary instinct for judging people and knowing what they can get out of them. They have a keen perception for social differences among the whites. With the rich they quickly adopt a flattering attitude, but they utterly despise the "poor whites." So long as they keep their place and are willing to sign, as it were, a declaration of everlasting inferiority, the South will admit that they are part of the family, and indeed more truly American than the

New York Jew or the Boston Italian. But let them try to climb socially, and they are looked on as dangerous beasts. In reality the South fears their progress even more than their brutality.

If the black zone could be surrounded by an impenetrable "sanitary cordon," the problem would be at a standstill in this enclosed space. Instead, however, a factor of enormous importance has entered into the situation with the recent migration to the North of part of the Negro population. In 1917, when industry was short of labour owing to war mobilization, the blacks deserted their native States *en masse,* attracted by higher salaries and the better social treatment which they hoped to find in the North. Also they were profoundly discouraged by their prospects in the South. The more or less cultured Negroes of the Atlantic States made their way to Philadelphia, New York, and Boston, while a primitive type went from Mississippi toward St. Louis, Chicago, and the great manufacturing cities of the Middle West. The two chief waves, one between 1916 and 1920 and the other from 1922 to 1924, involved some six or seven hundred thousand Negroes or more. There are now in the northern States almost a million and a half blacks, of whom a quarter of a million live in Harlem (New York) and 150,000 in Chicago. The frugal workman who earned from $1 to $3 a day on a plantation in Mississippi often gets $8 to $10 now in the industrial region of the Great Lakes. But his material prosperity does not help solve the race problem.

Having emancipated the Negro, the Northerners have always affected a kindly attitude toward him, partly on principle, but largely because they were never in direct contact. His sudden arrival in great hordes was bound to produce a serious crisis. Let us take for example what has happened in Chicago. First there was the housing problem. The newcomers camped down on arrival in the districts already occupied by coloured folk, and from there they spread to the neighbouring quarters. The invasion was peaceful but effective, and houses belonging to whites were soon entirely hemmed in by blacks. The occupants were disgusted, and gave way rather than struggle. Today an immense quarter stretching from the stock-yards to Lake Michigan is entirely coloured. Certain streets are 90 per cent. Negro, as is very evident to the passer-by. In the slums, in comfortable residences, and even in the former palaces of the newly rich, you see blacks at every door, at every window, and on every veranda. They swarm like flies.

The same thing occurred in the factories, and when the soldiers returned from Europe they found that in many cases their places had been taken by the intruders. The employers who saw in the Negro a useful strike-breaker took him on, not only for inferior positions, but even for skilled jobs. Trouble started with the jealousy of the foremen, who systematically relegated the Negro to the lowest positions. It was among the workmen themselves, however, that the resentment was most violent, and especially among those of foreign origin. The coalition against the black was tacit and spontaneous, and he was boycotted in the trade unions. Thus the whole life of the worker was jeopardized, for his trade-union solidarity was weakened to the advantage of the employer.

The atmosphere rapidly degenerated into a race war. In 1919 a chance incident, the murder of a black by a white and the refusal of the police to arrest the murderer, brought matters to a head. For several days there was an absolute reign of terror while the infuriated mob massacred the Negroes in a veritable pogrom. Peace was finally restored superficially, but daily intimidation still continues. Outrages are common, and the menace of a fresh crisis is latent. The poisonous virus of the South has penetrated only too well, and the danger is all the greater since the northern States have accorded civil equality to the Negroes. They are allowed to vote, their representatives sit in the local assemblies, their children go with the whites to the public schools, and mixed marriages are not forbidden by law.

What remains to be done to solve the problem? Legally very little, but socially almost everything; for a pitiless ostracism excludes the coloured man from all social contact. We must admit that the new experience in the North has only retarded the hope of a solution. Although theoretically well disposed, the Northerners are beginning to lose their old tolerance; for instead of merely giving free advice to others, they are now coping themselves with the difficulties of intimate contact. The Negro on his side endures this ostracism with growing impatience. As he becomes more civilized by city life his hostility takes on a bitterness and a hardness which the South never had to contend with, for in the North there are no hereditary sentiments to relieve the tension.

In the great cities of the North the Negroes are no longer the "good niggers" of legend, for they are neither humble nor deferential. In the economic struggle they have not fared so badly. In the factories they get good wages, they have their own newspapers, banks, and theatres, and among their *élite* are to be found lawyers, doctors, writers, and artists—a living proof of the fact that the race is able to rise. What more do they want? Their grandparents never dreamed of such progress, but at the bottom of their hearts they are longing not merely for civil equality but for social equality, or at least the theoretic possibility of social equality; and the tragedy is that they do not realize that it is impossible. "Are we not men?" the best of them will ask. "We are conscious of our merits. Why should we be treated as infectious pariahs? Or even worse, as if we did not exist?" Just as the South has always feared, they are basing their pretentions on rights, or a semblance of rights.

There are now two Negro questions, one in the South and one in the North; but the second reacts on the first. The coloured man who has lived in New York, and particularly if he has been to Europe in the army, frets under the traditional suppression. This opens up a new phase.

Though we must not take too seriously the Messiah-like movement for a return to Africa inspired by the agitator Garvey, on the other hand we must not ignore the fact that this American *élite* is strengthening the unity of the black race all over the world. Among these people a Negro who "passes" is a traitor, and a woman who marries a white is criticized, and if she becomes a white man's mistress she loses all caste. New York is the centre of this advanced Negro thought, but the South is also evolving toward it, either through outside influence or natural development. The wealthy Negro of the Cotton Belt, whose credit is better than the "poor white's" with the local banks, is a new factor in the evolution; but exactly how the Baptist and Methodist ministers will react is still a matter of conjecture. They are born leaders, however, and even when illiterate and undeserving they have great influence with the masses. There is a great gulf between the civilized Negro of Harlem and the husky brute of the Mississippi plantation, and obviously the solution of the problem cannot be the same in both cases.

An unprejudiced observer is forced to a painful conclusion. In the old days the whites may have been able to keep ten million men of another race under their yoke, but it is now very difficult and will probably be impossible in the future. What then are the avenues of escape? A return to Africa? The idea cannot be seriously entertained. The destruction of the race? Equally impossible. Fusion? This is occurring to a certain extent, but one hardly dares suggest it as a solution.

The only answer is that the whites must learn to live side by side with a race that they cannot possibly assimilate. However, they can comfort themselves with the knowledge that the percentage of blacks is diminishing. In 1920 there were 10,463,000 blacks out of a total population of 105,711,000 or some 9.9 percent., whereas in 1860 they comprised 14.1 percent. The reason is that though their birth rate is greater than the whites' (25.3 per 1,000 in 1922 against 22.2), their death rate is also much greater (16.3 as compared to 11.6). They die like flies in the cities into which they are pouring more and more rapidly. No doubt their death rate could be diminished by hygienic measures, but the southern whites look on such efforts with apprehension. On the other hand, if the Negro standard of living were improved, we must not forget that the birth rate would decrease somewhat. The fear of an irresistible tide of blacks can therefore be set aside as chimeric. Still, the ten million of today will be twelve or fifteen million tomorrow, and will not stop there.

Is the régime of yesterday and today to carry on?

"Yes," replies the South; "nothing else is possible."

Why not suppress the insults, recognize the Negro as a man, but maintain the separation of the races?

"No!" answers the horror-stricken South. "This very contempt is the best possible barrier, and once this line of defence had been pierced, we should have a hideous confusion."

No matter which way we turn in the North or the South, there seems to be no solution. The colour problem is an abyss into which we can look only with terror.

18: HARLEM AT THE ZENITH

*If you are walking absent-mindedly up Fifth Avenue,
and suddenly raise your eyes, you are surprised to
notice . . . a completely exotic picture. Within a few
yards, within a few minutes, the New Yorkers have all
turned black!*

New York's Harlem has always lured strangers from the United States
and abroad to see the lifestyles in America's largest black ghetto. Paul
Morand (1888–1976), French diplomat, writer, and member of l'Académie
Francaise, visited the "black mecca" in 1929, at the height of the Renais-
sance and jazz club era. Morand was attracted to the night life. Although
his descriptions of the people are somewhat racist, his vivid remembrances
shed light on aspects of Harlem culture.

If you are walking absent-mindedly up Fifth Avenue, and suddenly raise
your eyes, you are surprised to notice, in the accustomed frame of low
houses with brownstone fronts and front door steps, a completely exotic
picture. Within a few yards, within a few minutes, the New Yorkers have
all turned black! Or suppose you are in the subway, reading your newspaper.
The name of the station attracts your attention—One Hundred and Twenty-
fifth Street. Look round—your carriage has become a carriage of Negroes!
Clinging with long hooking hands to the leather straps, and chewing their
gum, they remind one of the great apes of Equatorial Africa. . . . It is
workaday Harlem, this, the Harlem of **domestic** servants, dish-washers,
laborers, cooks and elevator-boys, all going home. . . . Two stations further
on, the whole coach will turn white again, like day succeeding night. Above

Paul Morand, *New York,* translated by Hamish Miles (New York, Henry Holt and Co.,
1930), pp. 206–7, 267–75. Reprinted by permission of Hamish Miles, Jr.

ground, everything is games, shouts, rough-and-tumble. As there are no courtyards, the police have had to close certain streets to traffic so that the little Negroes can play hopscotch. Young Negresses, precociously mature, dash wildly along, swinging their bodies harmoniously, on atrociously noisy roller-skates, with an animal swiftness, a warlike zest, something savage and triumphant; they seem like the black virgins of some African revolution of the future. If you go up towards the Harlem River in winter, you find skating-places (as in every outlying part of New York), where the whole district is amusing itself by skating by arc lights after dark: there is a great beauty in these nocturnal glidings—the *délices mélancholiques* of skating beloved of Lamartine. One year after my stay in Timbuctoo, during the same month of February, I stand freezing as I watch this spectacle, so very un-African, of Negroes in sweaters and woolen helmets, cutting the ice with their swift, dark arabesques. The tropics in furs! Extremes touch hands: facial beauty-parlors, dandies in pink or green shirts, dealers in banjos or funeral wreaths (except for a Chinese funeral, there is nothing to touch a Negro one), Negroes endlessly chewing pellets of pepsin, with eyes lost in a far-away dream, in the grip of a mastication neurosis, mournful as Orientals fingering their beads; figures concealed in light-colored waterproofs (too light, indeed), fat cheeks protruding under hats too small.... Grouped together thus at the end of Manhattan, these blacks recover their sense of their identity and the quarter again becomes a place of exotic gaiety, of picturesque human confusion; they shatter the mechanical rhythm of America, and one can only be grateful for it; people had forgotten that men can live without bank balance, without bath-tubs. Standing erect at the street-crossing, symbolic of white civilization, the policeman keeps his eye on this miniature Africa; if that policeman happened to disappear, Harlem would quickly revert to a Haiti, given over to voodoo and the rhetorical despotism of a plumed Soulouque....

A Saturday night in summer, during the long-drawn July twilight, is the time to watch the Negroes, with their black heads gleaming and crinkly like mulberries, taking the air on their Lenox Avenue doorsteps, arguing and bickering and playing at their favorite game of "numbers," flirting with ornate words and simple eyes....

The apex of night-time Harlem came in 1926 and 1927. By 1929 its reputation was waning. Tired of the plantation decoration of "Cotton Club," "Sugar Cane," and "Second Part of the Night," I fell back on my friend Jupiter, a French Negro from Martinique and a stevedore at the docks. I started off by taxi in a real cinema snowstorm, and reached Morningside (four dollars on the meter) in front of the almost smart residence of my tattered Jupiter. Setting off together, we drew up (six dollars on the meter) at the door of a house which looked woebegone enough for my taste. At last—a Harlem unknown to Americans! The stevedore's friends were awaiting me in this hovel—in evening clothes; amidst these working-class streets they had fitted up a sordidly luxurious little establishment, with incense-burners, plush hangings, alabaster lamps, and a gramophone. Jupiter was very proud of his connections but rather shamefaced about himself, and left us very soon; he drifted away, very much the poor man, into the enveloping snow. But alas, my new acquaintances turned out to be unmistakably too "smart" for me; these Negroes were so much taken up with the glory of being seen with a white man that they showed me nothing, but showed me off all round. Already I could see the Cotton Club and the Sugar Cane looming up again. I protested. And we then went down into the African Room of the Harlem Club at 338 Lenox Avenue (no charge for cover, mural decorations by Aaron Douglas). We waited for the opening of a revue announced as "bizarre and varicolored," and meanwhile some little girls from Havana took seats at our table and fumbled in my pockets for spirits and letters of introduction in Paris. My companions were swollen up with pride, talked very loud, and in their dread of misusing the white language, used a much too carefully articulated idiom which attracted attention to us. . . . For all the syncopated murmurings of the Africano's company, the place was just like all the rest, Small's, or the old Nest, or the Savoy Ball Room, or the Capitol. Suddenly, one of the women who regularly frequented the place came up to me. She had observed me noting down some impression.

"I see!" she said, with a knowing glance. "Looking for some material . . ."

. . . .

In the underground cabaret to which I went on, there were a certain number of young girls in green and mauve dresses who were going to appear a little later in the "Bronze Beauties" revue. They were heavily painted and were having drinks in the company of some big black pimps whose woolly pates were adorned with patches of sticking-plaster. These gentlemen had had an argument in the street the previous evening, and the black policeman had given their skulls a few knocks with his leaded baton; tonight they had made the peace, and their powerful paws were stroking the bare backs of their dancing-partners, who, in quite a Berlin manner, were not girls at all. The waiter served the drinks, skating and sliding across the polished floor. . . . An old woman came in hiding a parcel under her arm.

"Hot stockings! Hot stockings!" cried the gentlemen-ladies of the chorus.

It was the hour for bargains in stockings, stolen during the day in the department stores and sold cheap at night. The "fairies" rushed forward, while a song of Helen Morgan's began to rise amid the thunder of drums and the jungle cries. . . .

Already a few cataleptic drinkers were being hoisted up the narrow stairs; already the blind old Negro who sells the morning papers was coming along, guided by a star of the establishment, and now one could read by daylight a large poster which announced—

Now come up to Harlem town:
See things done up hot and brown!

Harlem is the home-town of jazz. Jazz is the Negro melody of the South arriving at Pennsylvania Station and suddenly maddened by adorable Manhattan, where everything is noise and light. It is the Mississippi's dream become a nightmare, cut across by motor-horns and sirens; just as one is aware of the tumult of the elements beneath Wagner, so deep beneath Wagner, so deep beneath jazz one hears the mutterings of Lenox Avenue. The Negro is happy in New York. No hard work, no Ku Klux Klan, no Jim Crow cars. Right in the town, a Negro can now be served in popular restaurants. Many white schools admit his children, except when white parents protest. The more cultured have access to the liberal professions, and form a pleasant artistic center, a small "intelligentsia" in contact with similar white groups. It can count performers like Roland Hayes, the tenor; Paul Robeson, the incomparable actor of *The Emperor Jones* and the fine baritone of *Show Boat;* Walter White, the excellent Negro novelist (if one can say Negro, for White is as pink and fair as a Swede)—and others. It is through the medium of art or music or poetry that, during the past ten years, the respect and sympathy of New York has been forced by men like Countee Cullen, James Weldon Johnson, Braithwaite, by novelists like Fisher, MacKay, W. E. B. Du Bois, Nella Larsen, by painters like Aaron Douglas, Woodruff, and Albert Smith. . . .

The Negro theaters in Harlem—the Lafayette, Alhambra, and Lincoln— are not generally frequented by white people, except at the midnight show on Fridays; and this is one of Manhattan's curiosities. Europe has seen various Negro revues; they are always more or less compounded of the same jokes and the same broad effects; but the gesticulation of these actors—fawn or gray or chocolate-colored—seems to project a vital force into the auditorium; they seem to recharge the potential of their listeners. One never tires of the speed of their work, the violence of those colored comedians, the Negresses who let their notes fall like pieces of money, those singers who never sing flat, the elasticity of their tireless limbs, their jokes bursting like bombs, their laughter rattling like automatic pistols, and all the frenzied sequence of scenes. But what Europe cannot know is the audience itself—the beauties of Little Africa in their soft colored dresses like confectioners' jars, the shirt-fronts and the over-glittering studs of the bucks of a Hundred and Thirty-fifth Street. The comic, the sentimental, or the realistic scenes of the Negro theater have a truthfulness and humor that border on the sublime. Sometimes there are classical performances; and never shall I forget an *Othello* in which Desdemona, in her pink gown, was blacker far than Othello himself.

19: HARLEM IN THE 1940s

*Clamped to the heart of New York, Harlem weighs
on the good conscience of the white people in the
same way that original sin does on that of the
Christian.*

A distinguished French writer and educator, Simone de Beauvoir, traveled across the states on a lecture tour from January 25 to May 20, 1947. During the stay she spent some time in Harlem. Beauvoir laughed off the fears of her peers concerning walks in the black ghetto. Along with a couple of friends, including the black novelist Richard Wright, she enjoyed the world uptown, particularly the beauty and ease of the people. Her recollections present a different portrait from the one depicted by her predecessor, Paul Morand.

February 3rd: Of course I wanted to know Harlem, but it is not the only Negro section in New York. There is an important community of Negroes in Brooklyn, another (Jamaica) in Queens, and others, too, at the city boundaries: even in Manhattan itself you find sections here and there lived in by colored people.

Those who worship American power on their knees are even more servile than Americans themselves in adopting their prejudices. One Frenchman said to me: "If you like, we will drive through Harlem; you can motor through it, but do not on any account go there on foot." Another, who was bolder, said: "If you insist on seeing Harlem, at least do not wander off the avenues: if something happens, you can always take refuge in the

Simone de Beauvoir, *America Day by Day,* translated by Patrick Dudley (New York, Grove Press, 1953), pp. 34–40, 59–60, 299–301. Reprinted by permission of Ms. Ellen Wright.

subway; but avoid the side streets." And, trembling with fear, they told me how white people had been found with their throats cut in the gutters at dawn. But I had in the course of my life explored so many places where prudent people said one couldn't *possibly* go that I was not too impressed. I deliberately walked towards Harlem.

I walked towards Harlem, but my steps were not altogether casual; this was not just a walk but something of an adventure. Some force seemed to hold me back, a force, emanating from Harlem itself, which somehow repelled me: fear. But it was not my fear: it was other people's, the fear of all those people who never venture into Harlem, and who sense some vast, mysterious, and forbidden zone in the northern part of their city where they are changed into enemies. I turned a corner, and my heart stood still; the scene had changed completely. I had been told, "There is nothing to see in Harlem: it is an odd corner of New York where people have colored skins." And, indeed, on One Hundred and Twenty-fifth Street I found again the movies, drugstores, shops, bars and restaurants of Forty-second and Fourteenth Streets, but the atmosphere was as changed as though I had crossed a mountain range or an arm of the sea. There was suddenly a caterwauling of colored children, dressed in bright checkered shirts of red and green squares, and school children with woolly hair and deep brown legs, chattering away on the curb; the people were slumbering in doorways, while some sauntered about with their hands in their pockets; their relaxed features did not seem concentrated on some invisible point in the future but reflected the scene as it appeared then under the sky. There was nothing frightening; I even felt a growing sense of joy and an inner calm that New York had never given me until this moment. If, on turning a corner, say, in Lille or Lyons, I had suddenly found myself on the Canebière, I would have felt the same pleasure. But the change of scene was not just picturesque: there was nothing frightening about it, yet fear was there and weighed heavily on this great gathering of people.

Crossing the street, I advanced through layers of fear; fear inspired by these children with livid eyes, these men in light-colored suits and these women without haste. One Hundred and Twenty-fifth Street is a frontier: there are still a few white people to be found there. But on Lenox Avenue there is not a face to be seen that is not black or brown. No one paid any attention to me. The setting was the same here as on the avenues of downtown Manhattan, and these people, with all their indolence and gaiety, seemed no more different from the inhabitants of downtown than the people of Marseilles from those of Lille. One could walk down Lenox Avenue, and I asked myself just what I could have done to be made to flee from here, screaming, towards the protection of a subway station; it seemed as difficult to provoke rape or murder here as it would have been on

Columbus Circle at midday. Strange orgies must take place in the minds of serious-thinking people; as for me, this broad, gay, peaceful boulevard acted like a brake on my imagination. I looked into the side streets; there were scarcely more than a few children milling around on roller skates to disturb the quiet, *petit bourgeois* scene: they did not look dangerous.

I walked down avenues and in the side streets; when I grew tired, I sat down in the squares; nothing could happen to me. And if my feeling of security was not absolutely serene, it was on account of that fear in the hearts of people whose skin was of the same color as mine. If some rich businessman is frightened when he ventures into sections where people go hungry, that is understandable; he walks in a world which does not accept his own and which may triumph over it someday. But Harlem is a society on its own, with its middle class and its proletariat, rich and poor, unmelded in some revolutionary movement, wishing to integrate themselves with America, not to destroy it. These people will not suddenly roll forward in a flood heading for Wall Street; the unreasonable fear they inspire must be the reverse side of some hatred or remorse. Clamped to the heart of New York, Harlem weighs on the good conscience of the white people in the same way that original sin does on that of the Christian.

Among men of his own race, the American cherishes a dream of good humor, goodwill and friendship and even puts these virtues into practice. But they wither at the gates of Harlem. The average American, so anxious to be in harmony with the world and with himself, knows that beyond these barriers he assumes the hated features of the oppressor and the enemy; and it is this appearance which strikes terror into him. He knows himself to be hated, and this thorn in his conciliatory heart is more unbearable than any concrete danger. And all the white men who have not the will and courage to work for fraternity try to deny the very existence of Harlem and forget about it. It is not a threat to the future, but a wound from which they are suffering right now. It is an accursed city, a city where they are cursed, and, in fact, it is themselves they are afraid of meeting at the street corners. Because I am white, this curse weighs heavily on me also, no matter what I may think or say or do. I dare not smile at the children in the squares, nor do I feel I have a right to wander in the streets where the very color of my eyes typifies injustice, arrogance, and hate.

It was more on account of this moral uneasiness than of fear that I was glad Richard Wright was accompanying me to the Savoy tonight; I should feel less suspect. He came to fetch me at the hotel, and I noticed he was not looked on kindly by the people in the lobby; if he were to ask for a room here, he might be told that there were no more available. We dined at a Chinese restaurant downtown, for it was likely they would refuse to serve us uptown. Wright lives in Greenwich Village with his wife, who is white and comes from Brooklyn, and she told me that when she walks in the neighborhood with her little girl, she hears the most unflattering remarks. While we were searching for a taxi, people looked darkly at this Negro accompanied by two white women; there were taxi drivers who flatly refused to stop. After that, how could I hope to mingle quietly in the life of Harlem? I felt a kind of stiffness that made me feel guilty.

While Wright was buying tickets at the entrance to the Savoy, two sailors called out to Ellen and me, as sailors the world over call out to women at the entrance to dance halls, yet I felt embarrassed as never before; I should have to be offensive or else equivocal. But Wright, with a word and a smile, arranged everything; a white man would never have found just the right word and the right smile, and his intervention, though natural and simple, would only have aggravated my embarrassment. I climbed the steps with a light heart: Wright's friendship, his presence at my side, seemed to absolve me tonight.

The Savoy is a huge American dance hall, and in no way exotic. On one side the floor is bounded by a wall against which the band is placed; on the other side are boxes with tables and chairs, and beyond is a kind of hall like a hotel lobby. The floor is carpeted, and there are people sitting in armchairs, looking bored; they are non-drinking customers; they pay only to enter, and in the interval between dances women knit as though at a country dance. We sat in one of the boxes, and Wright put a bottle of whiskey on the table; whiskey is not sold, but patrons can bring it; we ordered soda water, drank, and looked on. There was not a single white face. Although this place is as open to visitors as Lenox Avenue, only a few jazz enthusiasts and foreigners feel the urge to venture there from downtown.

Most of the women were young, in simple skirts and short pull-overs, but their high-heeled shoes had sometimes the look of cloven hoofs; the light or dark tan of their skin suits their bare legs better than nylon stockings; many were pretty, but, above all, each was alive. How different from the strained coldness of white Americans. And when these people dance, their animal vitality is not choked by the armor of Puritan virtue, and you understand how sexual jealousy can enter into the hatred that white men in America carry within themselves. However, only a small percentage of lynchings, riots, etc., have a pretext of sexual basis. Although envy goes even further, it is said freely and without spite: "Those people are freer and happier than we." There is some truth in this. What gaiety, what life and freedom in all this music and dancing! It struck me even more in this dance hall, which had about it something of home and everyday life.

In Paris, when Negroes dance with white people in the rue Blomet, they are too self-conscious. But here they are among themselves; they have worked all day and have come in search of amusement with their boyfriends; they do not aim at creating an effect. Many of the young women belong to decent families and probably go to church on Sunday morning. They dance simply and in a way natural to them: one must relax completely to be possessed by the music and the rhythm of jazz: and it is also this relaxation which gives vent to dreaming, emotion, naturalness to a degree unknown to the majority of Americans.

Of course, the prejudiced pick an argument: why should one try to change the conditions for Negroes if they are happy and absolutely free? It is the old argument of capitalists and planters: it is always the workers, the natives who are happiest and most free. Although the oppressed escape the power of the idols which the oppressors have set up for themselves, this privilege is not sufficient to justify oppression.

I listened to the band, I looked at the dancers, drank whiskey; I was beginning to like it. I was feeling fine. The Savoy is one of the biggest dance halls in New York, that is to say one of the biggest in the world; there was something very satisfying in this. And the band is also perhaps the best in the world: at all events, nowhere else does it sound more authentic; the truth is there in the dancing, in the heart, in the whole life of the assembled people. When I listened to a dance band at home, when I saw Negroes dancing, the perspective was never altogether true; it suggested something different, a reality which might attain to greater fruition and of which it was but a doubtful reflection. But tonight I felt its message, I touched on something which was linked to nothing but itself: I had emerged from the cave. From time to time I felt that fullness of spirit in New York which contemplation of a pure idea gives to a freed personality; that was the greatest miracle of my journey, and it was never more dazzling than today.

February 9th: It was a fine frosty day. In the morning I went with Richard Wright to a church service for Negroes at the Abyssinian Baptist Church, the biggest in New York. It has between twelve and fourteen thousand members. The minister was a well-known popular figure, the Reverend Clayton Powell, young and ambitious. He was an intensive social worker and often helped workers on strike; he published a review for Negroes and was a member of the New York City Council. He was representative of a class of clergymen that is quite rare: those who devote themselves to maintaining and expressing the needs of the Negroes. I was struck by the social aspect of his sermon: indeed, you would have said it was less of a religious **gathering** than a political meeting. He reminded his Negro congregation of their hardships but said they would not improve matters by revolt or hatred; first they must win God's love, for there was also injustice among themselves: there were rich and poor, and they must learn to help one another in sickness and in health; let them come often to church, let their habits be pure, let them live for what is good, and then a day would surely come that would put an end to their troubles. The congregation listened with rapt attention and interrupted the sermon with cries of "Yes!" "All right!" while stamping their feet and clapping their hands at the same time, although it was a highly respectable congregation from the Negro middle class, which knew how to moderate its expressions. Wright told me that to hear the best spirituals and feel the emotional side of the Negro people's religion one must visit the churches in the poorer sections. He would take me there. The political, lay aspect of the service impressed me: one must understand, Wright said, that there is not a single minute in the life of a Negro that is not penetrated by a social consciousness: from the cradle to the grave, whether working, eating, loving, walking, dancing or praying, he can never forget that he is black, and this makes him conscious every minute of a white man's world whence the word "black" derives its meaning. Whatever he does, a Negro remains in "bondage." And there is not a single Negro writer who remains unaware of this problem of "bondage." They already know the answer.

. . . .

May 9th: So this was my last evening in New York. I would spend it in Harlem with A. E. and R. W. We dined in a Chinese restaurant and asked the taxi-driver to take us along the drive that follows the East River. Transformed by the night, Brooklyn and Queens glittered; the skyscraper façades were now translucent, the skies were gay with the reds and greens of neon signs. This was the last time I should see the fabulous landscape. R. W. was gay; he did imitations of a radio commentator at a baseball game and Dr. Anthony giving advice to troubled souls. When we stopped, the taxi-driver said admiringly, "Your act's great," and, determined not to be left out, he showed off the automatic windows of his taxi, which was the latest model.

In the first nightclub we entered the band was playing the new dance music which A. E. had told me about—be-bop. The band here played a jazz which did not follow the New Orleans' tradition but was only the breathless, exasperated expression of the fever of New York life. The room was empty; it was a "recession"; or was it that the public could not take these rhythmic storms? As a matter of fact, it was impossible to stand them for long, and we were limp with fatigue at the end of half an hour. The second club was slightly less deserted, the music was less trying; there were some cabaret acts, songs, and dances. One number had a great success; an elderly colored woman, fat and slipshod in a pink flannel bathrobe, with curlers and nightcap on her head, sang and told anecdotes in a raucous

voice. A. E. and R. W. said she was very funny; but her songs and her remarks, in a Southern accent, full of allusions and obscure double meanings,
meant nothing to me. The imitations amused me, and I liked the character-
izations, but I felt humiliated because I could not understand a single word.

We walked down Lenox Avenue. We were hungry and entered a "Bar-
B-Q" restaurant. I had seen this sign all over America. Barbecued meat is
simply meat cooked on a spit; this primitive way of cooking is thought
amusing in a land of electric cookers. We sat down at a little wooden table
in a tiny room where spits were turning on a grill behind a counter; chickens
and pork cutlets were impaled on steel prongs. The walls were covered with
photographs of boxers, dancers, and colored singers. There were joking
inscriptions, as in all popular bars, and we were struck by one: "If you
want your prayers to be answered, don't stay on your knees, get up and
holler." This was Harlem.

While eating pork chops and French Fries and drinking water—these
modest places have no liquor license—we returned, of course, to a discussion of the colored problem. R. W. especially deplored the kind of attrac-
tion white people in the North, and particularly in New York, feel for
Negroes. They define the Negro as the antithesis of American civilization,
splendidly gifted in music and the dance, rich in animal instincts (including
extraordinary sexual potency), careless, irresponsible, full of dreams, poetic
filled with religious sentiment, undisciplined, childish—such is the picture
they build up of the colored people. They go to Harlem because they have
projected onto the Negro what they themselves would like to be and
are not. But those who feel the greatest fascination are the people who really
sense the gravest deficiencies in themselves. These "nigger-lovers," as they
are called in the South, are for the most part embittered, diseased, neurotic
individuals, devoured by feelings of inferiority.

VII

STRUGGLES OF THE 1960s

... In the United States, scene of the latest outbursts of racial violence, the challenge to authority is spectacular rather than real.

Laurence Gandar, 1967

On December 1, 1955, a little black woman, Rosa Parks, was arrested for violation of a Montgomery, Alabama city ordinance prohibiting blacks from sitting in white sections of the municipal buses. The Montgomery Improvement Association and two black ministers, Martin Luther King, Jr., and Ralph Abernathy, came to her aid. Through combined efforts a year-long bus boycott achieved a major civil rights victory. By December, 1956, the black citizens of Montgomery had forced the integration of seating. A nation was to hear more from this episode.

The sweet taste of success in Alabama fueled the brewing black struggle, already livened by the Brown decision of the Supreme Court in 1954, calling for the integration of public schools. King and his southern supporters established the Southern Christian Leadership Conference in 1957 as the arm of the passive resistance movement.

The eyes of the world focused on SCLC and its dynamic leader as the South became a war zone of violent whites and passive civil rights workers. President Eisenhower's use of troops to enforce Supreme Court rulings during the Little Rock, Arkansas, confrontation in 1957 solidified an already embittered southern white population. Citizens Councils and United Klans organized protests to counter national policy. By 1960 white and black northerners joined the struggle to end segregation. "Freedom riders" in that year went south to aid in the sit-down tactics being employed by college students in North Carolina. Students were to establish the Student Non-Violent Coordinating Committee in 1961.

The movement reached new heights during the course of events in 1963. Martin Luther King, Jr., and 250,000 supporters marched on Washington, D. C., to dramatize to President Kennedy the need for federal civil rights and voting legislation. The situation in Birmingham, Alabama, was explosive. The bombing of a black church and resulting death of four little girls one month after the August march indicated that something had to be done.

Kennedy, of course, was not blind to the events. Before his assassination later that year he proposed legislation, later to become law in 1964 and 1965. Civil rights and voting protection were victories for the movement. Racists throughout the country, however, served notice that legal rulings could not stop ideas in the minds of men.

By 1965 conditions across the nation had worsened. Before his violent death in February of that year, Malcolm X, the black leader, late of the Nation of Islam and later of his own Organization of Afro-American Unity, announced to the world that it was either the "ballot or the bullet." Many blacks, suffering economic as well as sociopolitical problems, were impatient of the gradualistic tactics utilized in the southern campaigns. Northern ghettoes had further declined during the era. Civil rights gains never improved the decadent housing, job market, and generally pathetic conditions in Harlem, Watts, Huff, Roxbury, Newark, and other urban "jungles." These areas exploded between 1964 and 1967. Protests of the fifties developed into riots of the sixties. This violence extended beyond King's control. This he realized during his abortive attempt in 1967 to integrate Chicago suburbs.

The war in Vietnam had a telling effect on King: his philosophy broadened. King, always an advocate of human rights, now spoke for world peace and a war on poverty. His program changed to adapt to circumstances as he realized that the struggle was no longer for civil rights but for economic and human rights. The opponent was now the American system. Poor people marched for him now, not just blacks.

King was assassinated on April 4, 1968. He had already become an international symbol of harmony between all people. His life brought together young and old, black and white, rich and poor. His charisma captured the hearts of many. The movement died with him.

The struggle for Afro-American rights in the era 1954-68 was no revolutionary endeavor. Instead, it was a militant reform drive to incorporate black people into the system. Protesters, whether they were passive or riotous, signaled to America their needs, needs to be accepted as full-fledged citizens, no more, no less.

RAY KERRISON and ROBERT M. SHELTON

20: INTERVIEW WITH THE GRAND WIZARD
OF THE KU KLUX KLAN

"Niggers aren't fit to associate with us whites. They only shed their tails, like monkeys . . . , 200 years ago."

In the crucial civil rights year 1963, Ray Kerrison, a reporter for the Australian *Sunday Times,* came to the United States to interview the Supreme Wizard of the Ku Klux Klan. The conversation is included below.

Mr. Robert M. Shelton, the Imperial Grand Wizard of the Ku Klux Klan, was sitting in his wood-paneled, flag-framed office when he told me his favorite joke.

"Once upon a time," he began in his deep Alabama drawl, "there was a pretty young gal named Caroline Kennedy, who wanted to get married.

"She went to her mammy to tell her the good news.

" 'Who's the bridegroom?' Jackie asked.

" 'Martin Luther King III,' Caroline replied.

" 'You can't marry him,' said Jackie. 'He's a nigger. Go tell your father.'

"So little Caroline went to her father, the President. He asked her: 'Who will be your husband?'

" 'Martin Luther King III,' said Caroline.

" 'Impossible! Impossible!' he said.

" 'Why?' asked Caroline.

" 'Because he's a Baptist,' said the President."

Having thus scored his point about the "nigger-loving jerk" in the White

---

Ray Kerrison, "The Ku Klux Klaxon," *The Sunday Times* (Perth, Australia), June 2, 1963. Reprinted by permission of Mr. Ray Kerrison and *The Sunday Times.*

House, the Imperial Wizard—a lean, square-jawed, blue-eyed man of thirty-four who earns his living as a salesman of air conditioners for cars—went on to give his first interview to an Australian reporter.

As he did so, the race-torn city of Birmingham just sixty miles away was simmering.

It is a city with huge billboards calling for the impeachment of Mr. Earl Warren, the Chief Justice of the U. S. Supreme Court.

Its telegraph poles are spiked with signs reading: "The South Shall Rise Again."

Against this background Mr. Shelton spoke about his number one headache—the American Negroes.

"I shall always call 'em niggers," he explained.

"Now, you have never seen a rattlesnake that isn't poisonous. Well, niggers are the same—they're all poisonous.

"They're the laziest, dirtiest, unhealthiest group of spongers in the world.

"They won't work. They don't pay taxes.

"They form only 10 percent of the population but commit 50 percent of the murders and assaults."

Mr. Shelton, really warming to his subject now, went on:

"Niggers aren't fit to associate with us whites.

"They only shed their tails, like monkeys in the African jungle, 200 years ago.

"They have to be kept in their place and we're going to do it."

By "we" he meant the Klan, the Night Riders whose violence, symbolized by burning crosses, white robes, and masks, has been the shame of America for nearly a hundred years.

In influence and stature, the Klan is now reported to be at its weakest point in history.

"Not so," said Mr. Shelton.

"We're stronger today than we've ever been. We don't disclose our membership, but the politicians say we've got 60,000 members in Alabama alone. And we got the niggers licked. Every little edict passed by the Communist Supreme Court builds the white man's resentment that much more."

He interrupted himself to tell another joke.

"You know they are soon going to rename Washington—they're going to call it Cadbury's because it's 60 percent chocolate and 40 percent white."

It is difficult to tell whom Mr. Shelton dislikes the most—Mr. Robert Kennedy, the Attorney General, Dr. Martin Luther King, . . . or the late Mrs. Eleanor Roosevelt.

"I got a name for that Kennedy—Bobbysox," he said. "He's a hack. He has never tried a case in court, yet he is the Attorney General. He and his brother Fitzgerald are selling America out to socialism and ruin." (Mr. Shelton refuses to call the President by his first name. "I like dirty old Fitzgerald better because it suits him.")

Mr. Shelton considers Dr. King a "rabble-rousing nigger Communist." "Our basic problem is that the Communist conspiracy has taken over the nigger movement. And as for the old Roosevelt woman, she was the Jezebel to the African tribes." He added confidentially: "You know, she had nigger blood in her."

He also cares little for American congressmen. "They all tell us to integrate—but only two of the 800 politicians in Washington send their kids to an integrated school. I'd like to see that great liberal, Fitzgerald Kennedy, send his kids to an integrated school."

Mr. Shelton said the Klan had nothing to do with the bombing of a Negro home and motel which ignited the recent shocking riot in Birmingham. "We had a meeting that night," he said. "Would it make sense to start throwing bombs a few hours later? We've offered a $1,000 reward for the bombers. But I can tell you who did it—the niggers. They did it to get publicity and scare some more money from their friends up north."

Mr. Shelton, whose office is neat, modern, and lined with books, confided that one of his best friends was an Australian.

"She lives in Sydney," he said, "but I won't tell you her name because it might embarrass her. She is a cousin of General Wainwright of Corregidor fame. I got a lot of admiring mail from Australia."

As I left his office I commented on a huge red flag crossed with white stars beside his desk.

"The Confederate flag," I said.

"That," said Mr. Shelton, "is the flag of the United States of America." Near it hung Old Glory. I could have sworn it blushed.

21: SIT-IN TACTICS IN ALABAMA

*The Negroes' method of Gandhi-like non-resistance
is effective because terror can last but a few days
in a democracy. . . .*

The Swiss reporter Lorenz Stucki, son of a former foreign minister to
the United States, was impressed by the sit-in tactics of blacks amid the
storm of racist antagonism in Birmingham, Alabama, in 1963. His article
originally appeared in a Swiss weekly, *Die Weltwoche.*

One of those old jokes which, like certain cartoons, **never** grow stale,
tells of the Soviet Intourist guide who took his American visitor to a new
railroad station so that he could see for himself the tremendous volume of
traffic, a testimonial to progress. When, after an hour's wait, the first train
chugged slowly by, the American observed that he didn't think this was
any great indication of progress. The Russian replied crossly: "Well, look
how you Americans treat the Negroes!"

Once again this joke echoes around the world. Hundreds of Negroes,
including many children, have been arrested in Birmingham, Alabama.
White racial fanatics blew up the motel where the Reverend Martin Luther
King had been staying and set off bombs at his brother's home. Angry,
unarmed Negroes battled the police for hours in the streets after approximately 2,500 members of the Ku Klux Klan had gathered on the outskirts
of the city and whipped up their anti-Negro hatred with the customary rites.

Lorenz Stucki, "Rearguard Action in Alabama," *Die Weltwoche* (Zurich, Switzerland),
May 17, 1963; translation appearing in *Atlas,* vol. 6, pp. 99–100 (August, 1963). Copyright © by *Atlas* (August, 1963). Reprinted by permission of the publisher.

Once again, as at Little Rock and Oxford, the President had to send Federal troops into the South.

This latest incident serves to strengthen, in the minds of millions, the argument: "Well, look how you Americans treat the Negroes!" Stop getting so wrought up over the mote in our eye and reproaching us for "Hungary" or "Tibet" or "Algeria" or even for the racial fanaticism of the Nazis! Communist propaganda in particular has fastened with delight on the situation and is increasing its impact with photographs. I remember seeing one photograph in an anti-"Yankee" pamphlet in Cuba that showed a grim-faced white American police officer standing over a dead, or badly wounded Negro lying in the street. Only on closer scrutiny did it become clear that it was the photograph of a serious traffic accident! But now in Birmingham photographs have been taken that do not need to be faked.

And yet these photographs, even though they are not themselves deliberate falsifications, will create fake concepts in the popular mind. The history of race relations in the Southern states does more than prove that the Americans, like other Western nations, are not above reproach; it also reveals that American society, thanks to its constitutional and democratic structure, is at once able and willing to solve difficult problems that have grown out of the past and to bring evolutionary rather than revolutionary methods to bear upon them. The metamorphosis taking place in the South is proceeding slowly and calmly. Occasional local explosions like that in Birmingham are not spreading to adjacent communities, let alone creating a united front of racial hatred. The Negroes' method of Gandhi-like non-resistance is effective—and it alone can be effective—because terror can last but a few days in a democracy: when the fanatics resort to terror, their cause is lost.

Even in Birmingham, which has remained until now a stronghold of racial segregation, the Negroes had already won their battle with their aggressive non-violent tactics while the Ku Klux Klan was gathered and the bombs were exploding. The dramatic final act in which the hitherto peaceful Negroes lost their patience won't change this victory.

The operation in Birmingham was one of a series of breakthroughs achieved by tactics organized under the leadership of Dr. King—tactics against which the defenders of white supremacy have been unable to take effective countermeasures. The Negroes simply sit down, usually in the large department stores or bus stations which have restaurants or cafés reserved for "Whites Only." They quietly occupy all the tables and just wait. If they are not served, no white person can be served either. In addition to the sitdowns in the cafés and restaurants of these stores, a boycott has been instituted by the entire Negro clientele which leads many merchants to capitulate quickly to avoid heavy losses. If an owner holds out, he has to ask the police to remove the Negroes, who accept arrest passively. But almost at once others take their places and the whole performance begins again. In consequence the jails are rapidly filled to overflowing and TV and press from all over the nation converge on the town. Department store owners, businessmen, and public officials appear in a bad light and finally surrender because their opposition costs too much in money and prestige. Thus the first breach is created and other stores and businesses usually do not even attempt to offer resistance.

This has now happened in Birmingham, as it did previously in many other cities. But this is not all: in recent years many exclusively white schools—conditions vary from state to state—have been desegregated and Negroes have been elected to office or appointed by whites. With an ever-increasing participation in voting procedures, the Negroes are steadily increasing their political power.

These more or less quiet successes merit attention even though they do not produce such dramatic headlines as the much rarer cases where resistance to this steady progress erupts into violence. On the whole, the disintegration of racial separation in the Southern states is progressing, with astonishing speed and remarkable ease. But "astonishing speed" does not mean that the entire problem can be completely solved within a few years.

That there should be some resistance on the part of the whites should not astonish anyone, including us Swiss. We need only imagine what would happen if our half-million foreign workers were all Negroes and we had to "integrate" them completely into our society together with their wives and countless children. The Negro in the South, traditionally regarded as an inferior and a former slave, is, on the average, very different from the white man in his customs, mentality, and development, even though the emergence of a Negro upper class and the existence of a white proletariat tend to obscure these differences and even to intensify points of conflict between Negroes and lower class whites struggling to preserve their social superiority. Traditional Southern life, which has preserved much of its old-fashioned, contemplative, almost feudalistic charm in the rural districts and smaller cities, will be greatly altered by the integration of the races and American Southerners are not the only people in the world who cling to the old traditions and defend themselves against a change that is, to their way of thinking, bad.

More and more Southerners—apart, of course from the fanatics—are resigning themselves to the inevitability of this progressive development, even if they do not actually believe in its wisdom or in the moral preachments of Northerners, who say, "All men are created equal."

Obviously the ideal solution would be to bow to the inevitable and to work actively to bring it to pass. Then the integration of the races would not cause white standards to be lowered but Negro standards to be raised, as happened long ago in Western Europe during the "integration" of the proletariat, when the workers became bourgeois rather than the bourgeois becoming proletarian. A minority strives toward this end and it may be as important a group as the minority of its adversaries, the racial fanatics.

The decisive reason, however, that first and second class citizenship will be eliminated in the world's leading exponent of democracy and in our era of anti-colonialism is this: the overwhelming majority of citizens and their responsible political leaders are bluntly rejecting measures that tend to maintain human injustice, police rule, and terror—all of which would have to be used to permanently oppress a minority that has become self-confident.

22: PROBLEMS OF THE BLACK MIDDLE CLASS

*". . . The avant-garde of the Negro bourgeoisie
often feels the need to fall back on the warmth
and protection of other Negroes. . . ."*

Foreign correspondents in the twentieth century often focused their
reports on the development of the black middle class. Furio Colombo,
covering American news for the Italian weekly *Il Mondo,* evaluated the
progress of the black "elite." His account reveals the ambiguities and
frustrations of that class in 1963.

The controversy stirred by the West Side Tennis Club's refusal some
years back to admit the eldest son of Dr. Ralph Bunche served, if nothing
else, to illuminate perhaps the most delicate and subtle aspect of the Negro
problem in America and to remind the liberals so busy with the technical
and legal details of the battle for equal rights that the end of segregation
does not mean necessarily (or immediately) the beginning of integration.
There is a gelid no man's land (clubs and private schools, the thousands
of ways to "protect" a section of town from infiltration by Negroes, zon-
ing applied in such a way that Negro children admitted to integrated schools
—bound by the principle of residence and obliged in fact to live in a Negro
area—find themselves in a Negro school just as before) that can discourage
and demoralize even those persons (of both races) most sincerely motivated
by the desire for complete integration.

Furio Colombo, "Blackball at the Tennis Club," *Il Mondo* (Rome, Italy) May 21,
1963; translation appearing in *Atlas,* vol. 6, pp. 93–96 (August, 1963). Copyright ©
by *Atlas* (August, 1963). Reprinted by permission of the publisher.

Since the case involving Dr. Bunche cannot, because of his high position in political life, be considered typical, perhaps more light is shed by other situations among the young Negro bourgeoisie in areas not (or no longer) disturbed by open racial tension. Price Cobbs, for example, a kind of Negro Glenn Ford who is a doctor in San Francisco. "I had always thought that the commonest instances of racial discrimination occurred only, or at least most readily, in poor areas. Everyone knows that the frustrations of poverty are bad counsellors and that a poor white man will not overlook the slightest opportunity to get his own back at the expense of a poor Negro. Economic reasons (poverty and underemployment among the whites) are certainly not the least of the causes of racial violence in the South. But now that I live in a good neighborhood—and an upper middle class one at that (new, comfortable houses, lawns, garages with two cars)— I know that the problem doesn't end with money. I've known that since the first time they threw stones at our windows or called my children 'niggers.' We thought of moving, but other neighbors encouraged us to stay. In a certain sense we are an experiment and we still don't know exactly what is in store for us or whether our children's future will be better than ours."

Cobbs is an intern at the Medical Center of the University of California. "No, there is practically no discrimination at the hospital. But this doesn't mean that the problem of a Negro doctor putting his hands on the body of a sick white person has been solved. It's hard to say what I feel when they tell me a new patient is waiting and I'm about to open the door and I don't know what his reaction will be (after all, he's sick) when he sees my face." . . .

Another member of this avant-garde—and if what these people have reached is not exactly integration, it is certainly far beyond segregation— is Charles Bryant, engineer and researcher for the huge Lockheed firm. Bryant neither fled from the South nor adjusted to it. In the heart of Georgia he heads a research department with five white engineers under him, and he has built a beautiful home in "no man's land"—a zone not yet residential and neither black nor white. But Bryant knows perfectly well that he cannot enjoy in splendid isolation the privileged position his intelligence has earned him. As soon as he finished building his house the local Negro organizations announced a boycott of all stores practicing discrimination—in other words, most of the stores in Georgia. Bryant and his wife support the boycott, and so they are living in their lovely new home practically without furniture. The Bryants' enclave (the house is in the middle of a beautiful and fragrant Faulknerian forest) is not easy to hold. Bryant lives and works like a white man, but he is a Negro like each of the twenty million American Negroes whose emancipation is not yet complete. Within this difficult contradiction lies the equilibrium of his life as a member of the Negro bourgeoisie and as a young executive who, as an exception, has gone beyond the barrier of racial considerations.

The case of Bryant and his unpurchased furniture sheds light on another aspect of the Negroes' battle for civil rights and equality. A slowly emerging ruling class (professional men, white collar workers, and ministers of the various Protestant denominations) is looking for subtler weapons with which to wage its war, and it is aware of, among other things, the immense importance of economic pressure. The boycotting of stores is an example. After a countrywide boycott by Negroes, a chain the size of Woolworth had to give in and hire colored salesgirls. A few months ago the Negro communities in Pennsylvania became convinced that Philadelphia's most important daily discriminated against them in hiring trained workers. Through constant propaganda in the churches, Negro families were persuaded not to buy that paper, to cancel their subscriptions and to avoid using it for advertising purposes. Within a few weeks' time the newspaper had lost millions of dollars. This newspaper, which earlier had opposed the "don't buy" campaign with fiery editorials, invited Negro leaders to discuss "the terms of surrender. Ninety young Negroes were hired by its publishers and circulation returned to normal.

Campaigns like this, which require good organization and political maturity, are not easy both because it is sometimes impossible to get the poorly educated and frustrated masses to act as a group and because it demands in many cases truly heroic qualities for the leaders to attain position (if they are not ministers or professional politicians). When white society finally admits a Negro, it demands that at least he "behave like a white man" and that he drop his solidarity (in such bad taste) with other Negroes who have "made it." After all, a basic principle of American society (so vehemently gainsaid by their barrier erected by prejudice) is that everyone must by his own labor and effort create his own success and make his own place in life. That the new executive or professional man or teacher accepted on equal terms should turn around and continue to make common cause with the less successful masses of his own color is an irritant and an offense to the new community that has adopted the new free and equal Negro. This drama is summed up by Baldwin's question: "When will the whites stop believing that equality means my rising to their level and not, for example, the contrary, or at least a meeting at a halfway point? When will they stop congratulating me for finally having become not a man, or an American, but 'like a white man'?"

This split reaction to the problem, with the suffering it involves for the Negroes who have achieved a measure of success, is reflected in the remarks of the Negro judge James Parsons of Chicago. . . .

Judge Parsons (the first Negro to win a Federal Court judgeship) says: "My job is to be a judge regardless of the color of the persons who come before my bench. Oh, I know perfectly well that the majority of Negroes regard this as disloyal—to them I am breaking a kind of oath that is supposed to bind us. I am in no way troubled by this; in my position I feel I must ignore color and racial differences. Perhaps it's because I don't come from the South, perhaps because I haven't had a bitter life. Or perhaps because I am aware that being Negro is *one* of the dramas, not *the* drama, of man's existence. I know certain sections of Chicago where it is hard and even dangerous to be Italian, for example. The way I see it is that in the 300 years of American history, and particularly in the last fifty, the whole history of mankind, of his love, of his creative vitality that always manages to heal even the most horrible wounds, as well as of his defects, his prejudices, is being relived at an accelerated pace, and sometimes a violent one. But we have laws, and we have a moral conscience to impose upon the often painful and sometimes wild forces of history impinging upon us. Unlike those who preceded us in suffering and in hardship, we know how it will end, how it has to end. With this knowledge, we have good reason to go calmly about our work.". . .

There is something wise and profound in the remarks of the Negro judge. In America we can view the history of mankind, the whole history of the slow and painful developments which took place over the centuries, repeating themselves in a society that began from scratch to reach a level of well-being that man has never before achieved but yet without finding a cure for ancient and dangerous maladies. It is like looking into a telescope and seeing all these events flattened out, occurring simultaneously in a single picture—the convulsions of the world, the desperate desire for vindication which often takes mistaken directions. If it comes to a choice between optimism and pessimism, humanity as a whole, not just America, must make the choice. But everything here is more alive, more open, richer in developments and unexpected leaps (even at evil) and the nerves and fibers of the coming generation are in plain view and are constantly exposed to terrible wounds. Struck across the face by the denial of a room, a home, a place in a school, or membership in a club, the avant-garde of the Negro bourgeoisie often feels the need to fall back on the warmth and protection of other Negroes, letting up a little in the struggle, and prejudice wins new years of life. . . .

The Negro who, by his own intelligence and labor, has reached the middle or upper middle class (they are few, but their number is increasing) dreams of a normal life—that is, outside the ghetto—for himself and his children, but frustration or the mere threat of frustration through rejection or hostility on the part of white neighbors too often makes him stay where he is. Why should *he* be the hero in the vanguard, he and *his* wife and *his* children?

But his surrender has a chain reaction backward—children give up trying to go on with their studies, families cease looking for better schools and young Negroes tend to give up at the very moment when the struggle requires greater persistence, more strength, more deeply felt and reasoned dedication.

And the *status quo* is harsh for Negroes even in the affluent society, even in wealthy cities like Chicago and New York. Not only is the percentage of drug addicts and alcoholics alarming (there are many more drug addicts among Negroes than among any other group in America) but there is the two-faceted problem of Negro unemployment. It is estimated that in New York alone at least 80,000 Negroes of working age are permanently out of work and colored laborers represent about half of the nation's unemployed. Furthermore, every time unemployment rises, about two thirds of those affected are Negroes. On the other hand, too often they lack that push, that personal ambition, and that individual drive for a better education and a better, more secure job which are the keys to everything in an individualistic society like America's. But ambition has been undermined by fear, frustration, and the feeling that there is nowhere to go; that with or without a college degree it will still be a dog's life, so why not just let things happen as they happen. Then things happen badly and the vicious circle closes; the ancient problem is self-consolidated, like a tombstone on top of itself. . . .

In addition to the limited activities of a few intellectuals and ministers who prefer creating a political conscience over playing on religious fanaticism, to the bourgeois minorities who never give up and who hold their ground, and to—and also against—those responsible but moderate (sometimes, in the opinion of Negroes, excessively moderate) groups, other organizations have been forming over the past few years. They are politically vague and confused but strong enough to exercise a certain pressure. But in what direction? This new force does not seem to contain ideas capable of clearing the way for a new civilization, for progress. It is a matter, rather, of a reactionary wave at a peak moment of frustration among the urban Negro masses. The most striking example of those groups is, of course, the Black Muslims of Elijah Muhammad.

For 300 years doctor after doctor has leaned over the ancient wound America has borne in its body since birth (which represents, symbolically, mankind's most atrocious contradiction). And the doctors, from the freers of the slaves to Kennedy's cabinet, have not always been equal to the task. The best hope is the probability that, under the pressure of history and of human suffering, they will not tire of talking about the problem, studying it and investigating every possible cure. And the issue will be kept alive as much by the troubled consciences of the whites as by agitation on the part of the Negroes.

"This long debate may be boring," says Whitney Young, a Harlem organizer, "but for 300 years Negroes have been the object of special attention for the purpose of keeping them segregated and excluded. There is nothing wrong with the fact that they have now been the object of special attention for ten years running if the aim is to restore to them the rights of which they have been so long deprived."

23: LIFE IN NASHVILLE, TENNESSEE, IN 1968

White women, whether they know it or not, have
been conditioned to fear and dislike the Negro male.

In the fall of 1967 Elizabeth Jane Howard accompanied her husband,
a university instructor, to Nashville, Tennessee. They returned to England
after a four months stay. Mrs. Howard wrote this account of Nashville life
just after the assassination of Dr. Martin Luther King, Jr., on April 4, 1968.
The hypocrisy of the white population and the "madness" of race relations
disturbed her.

It is startling how much one's reactions to events are conditioned by
whether or not one has any first-hand knowledge of the places or people
that the events are about. Eight months ago, the news that Dr. Martin
Luther King had been murdered would have engendered feelings in me
principally of shock—of horrified *surprise* more than anything else—but
after a winter spent in Nashville, Tennessee, the element of shock at this
tragedy is rather horribly diminished.

Before living in a Southern state of America, I had some idea of what
Dr. King lived and worked for; now I feel I have far more of an idea about
what that most noble and gentle man was up against. Trying to think calmly
about it, I found myself repeating with savage bitterness: "So somebody
has gone out and shot him a nigger." This was a phrase I heard used (in its

Elizabeth Jane Howard, "An Englishwoman Saw Madness in the South," *Sunday
Telegraph* (London, England) April 7, 1968. Reprinted by permission of the *Sunday
Telegraph.*

future tense) three times seriously, and by different people during the four and a half months I spent in the South.

I went because my husband was invited to teach for the fall semester at one of the universities of Nashville. We arrived with very ignorant—and open—minds; indeed, my husband chose this particular university from several other possibilities because we'd neither of us ever been to the South, and he felt that we ought to find out about it.

Perhaps, we said hopefully to each other on our way there, perhaps the Southerners, both colored and white, have found some way to deal peaceably and fairly with one another, perhaps the situation will turn out to be perfectly viable, undramatically okay and therefore not talked about very much except when there is some isolated instance of brutality or violence. . . . Naive as these views may be, there is some advantage in going to a new and unknown place entirely without prejudice: you are not only most properly trusting your own eyes and ears; you are starting with them and, with care, they can continue to be all you have got.

Nashville is the state capital of Tennessee: it has half a dozen universities, forty-seven Christian sects, and is the headquarters of guerrilla training for the Black Power group. It has about 200 millionaires.

A great deal of the place is suburb: small, detached houses standing amid grass and trees; gardens and fences or hedges round them are rare, but the effect of space and privacy for each house is strikingly different from and better than any suburb I have seen in England. The distances for shopping, education, or work mean that nearly everybody drives: that is, all white people and a fair number of Negroes. I once tried to shop walking, and felt immediately like the vulnerable character in a Hitchcock film.

There are two local newspapers, three television channels and I don't know how many radio stations. None of these informs the Tennesseans at all about what is going on outside the immediate vicinity, except for short but regular paragraphs about Vietnam and a very occasional statement about such items as Britain devaluing. But they will know that Dr. King is dead, not simply because Memphis is only a three-hour drive from Nashville, but because, one way or another, very few people in this university town will be actually indifferent to the event.

In a society that wants above all things not to have to consider its component parts, that makes openly, or covertly, a different (naturally much-inferior) species of the Negro, that suffers, I think, a feeling of mass inferiority in relation to Northern Americans ("those dam' Yankees; the war isn't over; the South will rise again; a Southerner's worth two Yankees," etc.—all heard by my ears and never a joke), the assassination by a white man of a Negro who systematically and patiently gave the lie to all their coarse, abusive, contemptuous, patronizing, and downright disgusting views about his race will touch off many more emotions than grief. I can imagine a repeat celebration party being given by the person who celebrated Kennedy's assassination (his civil rights bill was not popular with some whites in the South).

But below—admittedly occasional—peaks of this kind of very frightening madness lies the bedrock of hysteria and prejudice, of bone-headed stupidity and sexual obsession (there is an extraordinary amount of sexual anxiety on the part of the whites about Negroes—very much on the "I make love, you perform, he rapes" basis). White women, whether they know it or not, have been conditioned to fear and dislike the Negro male. Illustration: wife of a university professor criticizing Olivier's film performance as Othello on the ground that he was too much like a Negro. "His walk! And the way he carried his head! Who *could* love *that?*" No Desdemona, she.

In trying to understand these general attitudes of white Southerners to Negroes one comes back to the have, have-not aspect of the matter. White people, very much on the whole, that is to say 95 percent of the time, are richer, better educated, have access to better social services, get the right side of what often amounts to a double standard of justice have more and better opportunities for jobs and so of course can do far more for their children, and so on.

In situations where the haves live side by side for generation after generation with the have-nots, the haves certainly become emotionally brutalized. I have heard remarks made about and in front of Negroes that make Marie Antoinette's irresponsible suggestion about cake seem merely a piece of harmless, if fanciful, liberality. Possibly, in an unconscious effort not to feel guilty about one's fellow creatures having the rough edge of pretty well everything, there is a natural tendency to depersonalize them, to turn them into something else: Negroes are different from white people, you see. How? It was simple for Marie Antoinette and Co.: poor people were rabble, not much above animals—everybody knew that. But the white Southerner today cannot be so bare-faced and simple. He is supposed to be living in a democracy; there was no constricting nonsense like that in eighteenth-century France. He has to be devious, merely imply the inferiority difference. Negroes' brains are much smaller than white men's; they are very simple people, best treated like children; they love me, because I know how to treat them! they're just longing for one person (me) to be loyal to; they aren't really capable of anything but simple, manual jobs . . . there is no end to the silly, nasty, dishonest propaganda that goes on and on.

Nauseating offshoots of this are the middle-aged ladies whose mythopeia prompts them to astonishing faded, jaded little accounts of their Youth and Gracious Living—with loyal, devoted mammies in the Great House—

Times have Changed, but they Remember. After one or two of these sagas, I realized that none, anyway of these particular ladies, could possibly have had the childhood they were claiming, but that they put up with each other's lies for the sake of indulging in their own.

But apart from the depersonalizing and the mammy talk there is, of course, fear. White people are always afraid of what might happen to *them* if Negroes revolted against the present regime.

The emotional brutalizing the whites have suffered from or indulged in entails the inability to conceive of a living, working equality of rights and opportunities with a hitherto underprivileged society. They have sunk to, or have not evolved from, a simple jungle law: themselves *or* others—it cannot be both. (Of course we have all heard about this before, but actually to encounter it, to find it going on in 1968 is very different from hearing and reading about it.)

Surely a well-endowed university with the reputation for being one of the best in the South must entertain and propagate greater liberality? After a very few weeks there these hopes were certainly damaged. The students that I met were horrifyingly liable to remarks like this one: "I expect you've noticed that most of the trouble with Negroes is in the North: *we* know how to keep them in their place." This was an example of the young upon the old, old subject and it would seem that Daddy had known and was going to go on knowing best.

Were there any students who did not state or condone the attitude illustrated? I met one: a graduate student from Memphis, a young man of twenty-four who I can honestly say was the *only* person we met born and living in the South whose attitude and feeling about Negroes was natural, humane, and honest. I am not saying that everyone at that university talked the standard racist rubbish on this subject; I'm saying that the ones I talked to about that did it to me.

And what about the faculty? I met one of them who said (but not to me and not in my hearing) that he could not find it in his heart to give an A to either a Negro or a Jew (it is safer to be liberal about one's illiberality —it gives people too much to get hold of, as it were). Another member of the faculty, when faced with a Fireside Chat (having your class to your house to discuss whatever anybody wants to talk about) found that his class included a Negro. He could not have a nigger in his house. ("Scratch a Southerner and you find a Southerner," my husband morosely remarked.)

Right: to do them justice, the whole class refused to go. But the damage had been done. The Negro knew why nobody was going to the Fireside Chat. If someone teaching in a respectable center for higher education behaves like that—and gets away with it—what is somebody colored, aged eighteen, and clearly very bright or he would never have got there (a Negro getting into that sort of university is the equivalent of somebody with a cockney accent getting a commission in the Royal Navy—you have to be bloody extra good to make it), what *is* this young Negro to think—of the institution, the people who teach in it, and the society that supports this situation?

Well, then; what about all these Christian sects? At a large party one evening, I was accosted by a young couple who said that they wanted to come and see me sometime about a problem (I can't explain this suggestion, it was simply made.) They said that they were practicing Christians; I don't think they told me what kind: their problem was that Negroes were not allowed in their church; they had protested several times about this, because they felt that Christ had not envisaged or intended such segregation; none of His teaching fitted this view and thus they felt that they had to *leave* their church and did I agree with them?

The points about this are that nobody else said anything of the kind to me, with the inference also that there really was nobody for them to say it *to:* they were falling back upon a total stranger.

I think it is necessary to say here that I am talking about a very reactionary—and *uneducated*—society. To teach Darwin in Tennessee was illegal until a very few years ago. I lectured once, largely about contemporary fiction in the English language, and the chief, indeed, almost wholesale reaction was "what a lot you *know*"—a reaction that would make any sane acquaintance of mine snort. This response came from people who taught, not people who were there to learn.

In the four and a half months we met a fair cross-section of white people in Nashville. We made only two lots of friends (excepting Northern importations—damn Yankees whom we'd known before) and with them, at least, we could argue, and did not have carefully to think before we spoke.

Even so, with one very intelligent man I remember a prolonged argument in which he was defending the progress of emancipation, and we were pressing him on what these freedoms amounted to. We could get no more from him than the following: ten years ago the Negro could ride only in the back seats of public buses; now, he could ride in any seat; he might not feel comfortable about it, but it could be done.

I have tried to confine myself to the positive statements and responses that we encountered during this short time. There is not room here for the lies, the lip-service to liberalism, the awful smarmy stuff that is an insult to any intelligence at all. I can't be bothered with it, in the same way that there is not room here to describe the sharp contrast in social circumstances between Negroes and whites that was immediately, and then continuously, apparent in Nashville.

Nobody living there could possibly give credence to the "it's all getting better all the time—all right really" stuff. Starting at the emotional top of the local pyramid there are the mad ones; the "shoot me a nigger, let's celebrate" ones. But then, and truly more frightening, are all those people who have genuinely been indoctrinated, and do not want to discover or change anything. They know, you see, that the Negro is a different (and inferior) creature.

But before we get too smug about this, let's remember that it is the attitude that very many men hold about many women: the rationalizations are equated with inferiority, and as anybody in the least interested in eugenics knows, you can breed and condition people to almost anything.

So: the untimely, disastrous tragic death of Dr. King has what effect in Tennessee? The young Black Power group are going to say that they *told* everybody so: what good could an old-fashioned, liberal Uncle Tom expect to do? They may, nonetheless, try to use Dr. King as a martyr: but other people will do that anyway: anybody who dies during the process of working without violence for a goal such as his exposes himself to this accolade or imprecation.

Not the least homage that should be paid to Dr. King is that he knew for many years that he was continuously vulnerable to the possibility of murder. A madman, many white Southern people will say, and of course they will be right; only a madman would have done something so violently silly. They haven't thought that this act stems from many years and thousands of people whose attitude on this subject, to say the least, has not really ever been sane. It is this chronic bulk of hysterical prejudice and fear that has made such an assassination possible.

Nevertheless, the act *is* a violently silly one. Leaving aside what many people may have thought about Dr. King in particular and what they have thought or now think about the racial problems in the United States in general, the fact remains that the repercussions of what could be considered as the homicidal and antisocial act of some individual maniac are likely to be world-wide for a long time to come.

But it seems to me necessary to make the possibly simple point that these maniacs—effective maniacs, at least—are very unlikely to stem from some social vacuum: if it takes all sorts to make a world, it takes certain sorts to make certain bits of it. Looking back on our time in Nashville, the most depressing conclusions are that this murder does not startle us, and that we can think of only three persons there whose reactions to it we would call honest, unhappy, and sane.

BIBLIOGRAPHY

GENERAL

Thousands of foreign critiques and impressions of American society have been published since the seventeenth century. Foreign literature commenting exclusively on Afro-American life is not vast, but many observers examined race relations in the course of their travels.

A few general biographical collections were used for background material on different observers included in this study. These sources are abbreviated as follows:

DNB: Dictionary of National Biography (London, Smith, Elder and Co., 1888) and supplements to the original collection.

WBD: Webster's Biographical Dictionary (Springfield, Mass., G. and C. Merriam Co., 1972).

Among the most recent collections of foreign views of America are Henry Steele Commager and Elmo Giordanetti, eds., *Was America a Mistake? An Eighteenth Century Controversy* (New York, Harper & Row, 1967); Alan Westin, Julian Franklin, et al., eds., *Views of America* (New York, Harcourt, Brace & World, 1966); G. D. Lillibridge, ed., *The American Image: Past and Present* (Boston, D. C. Heath & Co., 1968) and Gerald Stearn, *Broken Image: Foreign Critiques of America* (New York, Random House, 1972). Alton Hornsby's *In the Cage: Eyewitness Accounts of the Freed Negro in Southern Society, 1877-1929* (Chicago, Quadrangle, 1971) is a good collection concentrating on the black experience, including many American views.

The Harvard Guide to American History (Cambridge, Harvard University Press, 1963) has an exhaustive list of travelers' works.

Biographical information about early European visitors was also taken from J. L. Mesick, *The English Traveller in America, 1795-1835* (New York, Columbia University Press, 1922); Frank Monaghan, *The French*

Travellers in the United States, 1765-1932 (New York, 1933), and Durrand Echeverria, *Mirage in the West: A History of the French Image of American Society to 1815* (Princeton University Press, 1968).

UNKNOWN DESTINY: THE SLAVE TRADE

Life sketches of the slave traders are scarce. See G. R. Crone's introduction to *The Voyages of Cadamosto and Other Documents on Western Africa in the Second Half of the Fifteenth Century* (London, 1937) for background material on Alvise da Cadamosto. The *DNB* has some information on Falconbridge. Sources on the slave trade and Africa abound. A few of the vivid memoirs include Willem Bosman's *A New and Accurate Description of the Coast of Guinea* (London, 1705); Thomas Winterbottom, *An Account of the Native Africans in the Neighborhood of Sierra Leone* (London, 1803), the recollections of a ship's surgeon in 1796, and Nicholas Owen, *Journal of a Slave Dealer* (Boston, 1930).

Major studies of the subject are Katherine George, "The Civilized West Looks at Primitive Africa: 1400–1800: A Study in Ethnocentrism," *Isis* 49 (1958); James Pope-Hennessy, *Sins of the Fathers: A Study of the Atlantic Slave Traders* (New York, Capricorn Books, 1969); Basil Davidson, *Black Mother* (Boston, Little Brown, 1961); and Daniel Mannix and Malcolm Cowley, *Black Cargoes* (New York, Viking Press, 1965).

SLAVERY

In addition to *WBD* check Durrand Echeverria's *Mirage in the West* for material on Crèvecoeur and the duc de la Rochefoucauld-Liancourt. The *Biographie Nouvelle des Contemporains*, vol. 18 (Paris, La Libraire Historique, 1825) includes a contemporary survey of the duke's accomplishments. *WBD* and *Who's Who in 1907* (London, A. and C. Black, 1907) are sketchy on Russell's background.

The slave experience, more than any other facet of black life, received close scrutiny by foreigners. Out of the quantity of literature the following are just a few of the classic observations: Alexis de Tocqueville, *Democracy in America* (London, Saunders and Otley, 1835), Frances Anne Kemble, *Journal of a Residence on a Georgia Plantation, 1838-1839* (New York, Harper and Brothers, 1863), and Charles Dickens, *American Notes* (New York, Harper and Brothers, 1842).

QUASI-FREE BLACKS

For Thomas Hamilton's life and attitudes see the *DNB* and Mesick's *English Traveller.* Alvin L. Tinnin's introduction to Beaumont's *Marie, or, Slavery in the United States* (Stanford University Press, 1958), translated by Barbara Chapman, mentions the Frenchman's life. George W. Pierson's *Tocqueville and Beaumont in America* (New York, Oxford University Press, 1938) is a thorough study. A short note on Lieber is in *Who*

Was Who in America, 1607-1896 (Chicago, Marquis Publications, 1963).
Some contemporary foreign writers in addition to those cited who
elaborate on the free black experience are Frances Trollope, *Domestic
Manners of the Americans* (London, 1832); George Lewis, *Impressions
of American and the American Churches* (Edinburgh, 1845); and Edward
Dicey, *Six Months in the Federal States* (London, 1863).

POSTBELLUM AGRARIAN LIFE

See the *DNB, First Supplement to 1900,* for Campbell, and the *Fourth
Supplement, 1922-32,* about Bryce.
Hundreds of Europeans toured the states after the Civil War to see the
condition of the freed slaves and the state of affairs of the strife-torn society. The English in particular were curious of any changes in racial and social
matters. Among the numerous British views see William H. Dixon, *New
America* (London, 1869); Sir John Kennaway, *On Sherman's Track, or
the South After the War* (London, 1867); Henry Latham, *Black and White:
A Journal of a Three Months' Tour in the United States* (London, 1867);
David Macrae, *Amongst the Darkies, and Other Papers* (Glasgow, 1876);
and F. B. Zinke's *Last Winter in the United States* (London, 1868).
For the early twentieth century see H. G. Wells's candid interview with
Booker T. Washington and W. E. B. Du Bois in that author's *The Future
in America: A Search after Realities* (New York, Harper and Brothers,
1906). Thomas Young, *The American Cotton Industry: A Study of Work
and Workers* (London, Methuen, 1902), and Iza Duffy Hardy, *Oranges and
Alligators: Sketches of South Florida Life* (London, Ward and Downey,
1886), describe southern black life.

THE GOSPEL OF JIM CROW

Details of Clowes's life appear in *WBD* and the *DNB, Second Supple-
ment, 1902-11,* vol. 1. *Who's Who, 1955* (London, Adam and Charles
Black, 1956) contains material on Klein.
The Scottish visitor William Archer concentrated on black life in his
Through Afro-America: An English Reading of the Race Problem (London,
Chapman and Hall, 1910). The Hungarian Count Vay De Vaya und Luskod's
The Inner Life of the United States (London, John Murray, 1908) has
bits of information.
Foreign critics often joined in the racist condemnation of blacks during
the jim crow era. Bitter ideas were advocated by Knut Hamsun in *The
Cultural Life of Modern America,* edited and translated by Barbara Gordon
Morgridge (Cambridge, Harvard University Press, 1969). In this realm is
Lepel Henry Griffin's *The Great Republic* (London, Chapman and Hall,
1884). Cesare Lombroso is blatant in "Why Homicide Has Increased in
the United States," *North American Review* 145 (December, 1897).

URBANIZATION

Refer to *Who's Who in France, 1959-1960* (Paris, Jacques Lafitte, 1959) and *WBD* for background on André Siegfried. See James Ethridge and Barbara Kopala, eds., *Contemporary Authors,* vols. 11-12 (Detroit, Gale Research Co., 1965), for Simone de Beauvoir's career. José Marti's vivid recollections of Charleston, South Carolina black life in 1886 have been collected and translated by Juan de Onis in *The America of José Marti* (New York, Noonday Press, 1954). Ethel Mannin recalls her trip in 1966 to Washington, D. C., in *An American Journey* (London, Hutchinson and Co., 1967).

STRUGGLES OF THE 1960s

Atlas magazine, an English language monthly of world news viewpoints, devoted extensive space to the coverage of race relations in America in the turbulent 1960s. Short biographical sketches appear for the foreign correspondents, including Kerrison, Stucki, Colombo, and Howard.

See also "The Negro Problem in the U.S.: An Outsider's View," *Monthly Review,* vol. 15 (1963), by Keith Buchanan. A massive recent study of the nation by an Englishman, Robert Hargreaves, is *Superpower: A Portrait of America in the 1970s* (New York, St. Martin's Press, 1973).

AUTHOR INDEX

TITLE INDEX